Modern Critical Interpretations

Leo Tolstoy's
Anna Karenina

Modern Critical Interpretations

These and other titles in preparation

Modern Critical Interpretations

Leo Tolstoy's
Anna Karenina

Edited and with an introduction by

Harold Bloom
Sterling Professor of the Humanities
Yale University

Chelsea House Publishers ◊ *1987*

NEW YORK ◊ NEW HAVEN ◊ PHILADELPHIA

© 1987 by Chelsea House Publishers, a division
of Chelsea House Educational Communications, Inc.
95 Madison Avenue, New York, NY 10016
345 Whitney Avenue, New Haven, CT 06511
5014 West Chester Pike, Edgemont, PA 19028

Introduction © 1987 by Harold Bloom

Printed and bound in the United States of America

10 9 8 7 6 5 4 3 2 1

∞ The paper used in this publication meets the minimum requirements
of the American National Standard for Permanence of Paper for Printed
Library Materials, Z39.48-1984.

Library of Congress Cataloging-in-Publication Data
Leo Tolstoy's Anna Karenina.
    (Modern critical interpretations)
    Bibliography: p.
    Includes index.
    Summary: Selections of literary criticism on Tolstoy's Anna Karenina.
    1. Tolstoy, Leo, graf, 1828–1910. Anna Karenina. [1. Tolstoy, Leo,
graf, 1828–1910. Anna Karenina. 2. Russian literature—History and
criticism] I. Bloom, Harold. II. Title. III. Series.
PG3365.A63B55   1987   891.73'3   87–11794
ISBN 1-55546-077-1 (alk. paper)

Contents

Editor's Note

This book brings together a representative selection of the best modern critical interpretations of Leo Tolstoy's novel *Anna Karenina*. The critical essays are reprinted here in the chronological order of their original publication. I am grateful to Neil Bermel for his assistance in editing this volume.

My introduction centers upon Anna as an embodiment of Schopenhauer's Will to Live. John Bayley begins the chronological sequence by considering Tolstoy's projected scenarios for *Anna Karenina* and then reflects that the complete novel, unlike the scenarios, contains "no truths, only people."

The relation between chance and fatality in *Anna Karenina* is explored by Robert Louis Jackson, after which Willis Konick studies conflicting visions of the heroine. That the book is two novels, Anna's and Levin's, is argued by Edward Wasiolek, who identifies Tolstoy's design or intentions with his accomplishment.

Maire Jaanus Kurrik emphasizes the self's negativity in *Anna Karenina*, particularly in Anna's relationship to her own body. In this book's final essay, Martin Price analyzes Tolstoy's moral imagination at work, testing the destructiveness of the exceptional individual's attempt to survive outside "the forms of life" and showing through Anna Karenina's suicide the "inexorable law" that dooms the fiercest exemplars of the will to live.

Introduction

Schopenhauer's fierce vision of the ravening Will to Live found a receptive sharer in Tolstoy, whose ferocious drives hardly needed guidance from Schopenhauer. *Anna Karenina* can be called the novel of the drives, since no other narrative that I have read centers so fully upon its protagonist's being so swept away by her will to live that almost nothing else matters to her. Anna's love for Vronsky may have its few rivals in Western literature, but I can recall no similar representation of erotic passion quite so intense. Tolstoy, with enormous shrewdness, explains nothing about Anna's object-choice to us, whether in idealizing or in reductive terms. What he does show us, with overwhelming persuasiveness, is that there is no choice involved. Anna, vital and attractive in every way, is someone with whom most male readers of the novel fall in love, and Tolstoy clearly loves her almost obsessively. He would not have said that he *was* Anna, but she resembles him rather more than Levin does, let alone Vronsky or Kitty.

Why does Anna kill herself? Would we find it as plausible if a contemporary Anna emulated her? Could there be a contemporary Anna? The questions may reduce to: Why did Tolstoy kill her? Did he mean to punish her? I think not. Anna's suicide saddens us, but it also relieves us from shared suffering. Doubtless it relieved Tolstoy also, who was suffering with her. Other legitimate questions would be: How would Schopenhauer have received Anna's death? Is it an heroic release, or a failure in endurance?

Tolstoy read Schopenhauer in the interval between *War and Peace* and *Anna Karenina*, an uneasy interregnum in which he was defeated by his attempt to write a novel about the era of Peter the Great. His enthusiasm for Schopenhauer was essentially a reaffirmation of his own darkest convictions, since he had always been both an apocalyptic vitalist and a dark moralist appalled by some of the consequences of his own vitalism. Schopenhauer's Will to Live, with its metaphysical status as the true thing-in-itself, is simply the Tolstoyan natural ethos turned into prose. The Will to Live is unitary,

1

active, rapacious, indifferent, universal desire; one of the most extraordinary of nineteenth-century hyperboles:

> Let us now add the consideration of the human race. The matter indeed becomes more complicated, and assumes a certain seriousness of aspect; but the fundamental character remains unaltered. Here also life presents itself by no means as a gift for enjoyment, but as a task, a drudgery to be performed; and in accordance with this we see, in great and small, universal need, ceaseless cares, constant pressure, endless strife, compulsory activity, with extreme exertion of all the powers of body and mind. Many millions, united into nations, strive for the common good, each individual on account of his own; but many thousands fall as a sacrifice for it. Now senseless delusions, now intriguing politics, incite them to wars with each other; then the sweat and the blood of the great multitude must flow, to carry out the ideas of individuals, or to expiate their faults. In peace industry and trade are active, inventions work miracles, seas are navigated, delicacies are collected from all ends of the world, the waves engulf thousands. All strive, some planning, others acting; the tumult is indescribable. But the ultimate aim of it all, what is it? To sustain ephermeral and tormented individuals through a short span of time in the most fortunate case with endurable want and comparative freedom from pain, which, however, is at once attended with ennui; then the reproduction of this race and its striving. In this evident disproportion between the trouble and the reward, the will to live appears to us from this point of view, if taken objectively, as a fool, or subjectively, as a delusion, seized by which everything living works with the utmost exertion of its strength for something that is of no value. But when we consider it more closely, we shall find here also that it is rather a blind pressure, a tendency entirely without ground or motive.

If this is the characterization of the Will to Live, then the metaphysics of the love of the sexes will reduce to a kind of treason:

> In between, however, in the midst of the tumult, we see the glances of two lovers meet longingly: yet why so secretly, fearfully, and stealthily? Because these lovers are the traitors who seek to perpetuate the whole want and drudgery, which would otherwise speedily reach an end; this they wish to frustrate, as others like them have frustrated it before.

Schopenhauer presumably would have found this exemplified as much by Levin and Kitty as by Vronsky and Anna, but there he and Tolstoy part, as even Tolstoy is a touch saner upon the metaphysics of sexual love. What matters most about Anna, at least to the reader, is her intensity, her will to live (I deliberately remove the Schopenhauerian capitalization). Anna's aura renders her first meeting with Vronsky unforgettable for us:

> Vronsky followed the guard to the carriage, and had to stop at the entrance of the compartment to let a lady pass out.
>
> The trained insight of a Society man enabled Vronsky with a single glance to decide that she belonged to the best Society. He apologized for being in her way and was about to enter the carriage, but felt compelled to have another look at her, not because she was very beautiful nor because of the elegance and modest grace of her whole figure, but because he saw in her sweet face as she passed him something specially tender and kind. When he looked round she too turned her head. Her bright grey eyes which seemed dark because of their black lashes rested for a moment on his face as if recognizing him, and then turned to the passing crowd evidently in search of some one. In that short look Vronsky had time to notice the subdued animation that enlivened her face and seemed to flutter between her bright eyes and a scarcely perceptible smile which curved her rosy lips. It was as if an excess of vitality so filled her whole being that it betrayed itself against her will, now in her smile, now in the light of her eyes. She deliberately tried to extinguish that light in her eyes, but it shone despite of her in her faint smile.

A benign vitality, however excessive, is what Tolstoy recognized in himself. What he teaches himself in this novel is that a vitality so exuberant transcends benignity as it does every other quality. The brief but overwhelming chapter 11 of part 2 is not only the novel in embryo, and the essence of Anna, but it is also, to me, the most revelatory scene that Tolstoy ever wrote:

> That which for nearly a year had been Vronsky's sole and exclusive desire, supplanting all his former desires: that which for Anna had been an impossible, dreadful, but all the more bewitching dream of happiness, had come to pass. Pale, with trembling lower jaw, he stood over her, entreating her to be calm, himself not knowing why or how.
>
> "Anna, Anna," he said in a trembling voice, "Anna, for God's sake! . . ."

But the louder he spoke the lower she drooped her once proud, bright, but now shame-stricken head, and she writhed, slipping down from the sofa on which she sat to the floor at his feet. She would have fallen on the carpet if he had not held her.

"My God! Forgive me!" she said, sobbing and pressing Vronsky's hand to her breast.

She felt so guilty, so much to blame, that it only remained for her to humble herself and ask to be forgiven; but she had no one in the world now except him, so that even her prayer for forgiveness was addressed to him. Looking at him, she felt her humiliation physically, and could say nothing more. He felt what a murderer must feel when looking at the body he has deprived of life. The body he had deprived of life was their love, the first period of their love. There was something frightful and revolting in the recollection of what had been paid for with this terrible price of shame. The shame she felt at her spiritual nakedness communicated itself to him. But in spite of the murderer's horror of the body of his victim, that body must be cut in pieces and hidden away, and he must make use of what he has obtained by the murder.

Then, as the murderer desperately throws himself on the body, as though with passion, and drags it and hacks it, so Vronsky covered her face and shoulders with kisses.

She held his hand and did not move. Yes! These kisses were what had been bought by that shame! "Yes, and this hand, which will always be mine, is the hand of my accomplice." She lifted his hand and kissed it. He knelt down and tried to see her face, but she hid it and did not speak. At last, as though mastering herself, she sat up and pushed him away. Her face was as beautiful as ever, but all the more piteous.

"It's all over," she said. "I have nothing but you left. Remember that."

"I cannot help remembering what is life itself to me! For one moment of that bliss . . ."

"What bliss?" she said with disgust and horror, and the horror was involuntarily communicated to him. "For heaven's sake, not another word."

She rose quickly and moved away from him.

"Not another word!" she repeated, and with a look of cold despair, strange to him, she left him. She felt that at that moment she could not express in words her feeling of shame, joy, and horror at this entrance on a new life, and she did not wish to vulgarize that feeling by inadequate words. Later on, the next day and the next, she still could not even find words to describe all the complexity of those feelings, and could not even find thoughts with which to reflect on all that was in her soul.

She said to herself: "No, I can't think about it now; later, when I am calmer." But that calm, necessary for reflection, never came. Every time the thought of what she had done, and of what was to become of her and of what she should do, came to her mind, she was seized with horror and drove these thoughts away.

"Not now; later, when I am calmer!" she said to herself.

But in her dreams, when she had no control over her thoughts, her position appeared to her in all its shocking nakedness. One dream she had almost every night. She dreamt that both at once were her husbands, and lavished their caresses on her. Alexey Alexandrovich wept, kissing her hands, saying: "How beautiful it is now!" and Alexey Vronsky was there too, and he also was her husband. And she was surprised that formerly this had seemed impossible to her, and laughingly explained to them how much simpler it really was, and that they were both now contented and happy. But this dream weighed on her like a nightmare, and she woke from it filled with horror.

Abruptly, without even an overt hint of the nature of the consummation, Tolstoy places us after the event. Anna's tragedy, and in some sense Tolstoy's own, is implicit in this majestic scene. Poor Vronsky, at once victim and executioner, is hopelessly inadequate to Anna's intensity. There is of course nothing he can say and nothing he can do, because he is the wrong man, and always will be. But who could have been the right man? Levin? Perhaps, but Tolstoy and life (the two are one) would not have it so. The calm, necessary for reflection, might have come to Anna with Levin, yet that is highly doubtful. Tolstoy himself, her double and brother, her psychic twin, would have been inadequate to Anna, and she to him. Anna's dream, with both Alexeys happy as her joint husbands, is a peculiar horror to her, because it so horrified Tolstoy. The outrage expressed by D. H. Lawrence at what he judged to be Tolstoy's murder of Anna might have been mitigated had Lawrence allowed himself to remember that Tolstoy, nearly thirty-five years after Anna, also died in a railroad station.

"Characters like Anna are tragic figures because, for reasons that are admirable, they cannot live divided lives or survive through repression." That sentence of Martin Price's is the best I have read about Anna, but I wonder if Anna can be called a tragic figure, any more than she can be what Schopenhauer grimly would have called her, a traitor. Tragedy depends upon division and repression, and Anna is betrayed by nature itself, which does not create men as vital as herself, or, if it does, creates them as savage moralists, like Tolstoy. Anna is too integral for tragedy, and too imbued with reality to survive in any social malforming of reality whatsoever. She dies because Tolstoy could not sustain the suffering it would have cost him to imagine a life she could have borne to go on living.

Anna Karenina

John Bayley

What may be Tolstoy's first draft [of *Anna Karenina*] begins quite differently from the finished novel, and may well have been intended as its opening scene. Its first sentence recalls the phrase of Pushkin. "After the opera, the guests gathered at the house of young Princess Vrasski." The party is like that given by Princess Betsy in chapter 7 of *Anna*, except that the host and hostess are young instead of middle-aged. Kitty is mentioned, and the hostess wonders aloud if something hasn't occurred between her and Anna. Vronsky (also referred to as Gagin) is known to be in love with Kitty, and the suggestion is that Anna may be trying to take him away from her. Conversation is barbed and allusive. "Naturally they talked of persons known to them all, and, equally naturally, they talked scandal about them: there would have been nothing to say otherwise, since happy people have no history." The hostess says that Anna is certainly not attractive, but that she would fall for her if she were a man. A diplomat remarks that now or never is her moment to become the heroine of a novel.

Stiva enters, already recognisable, but his opening dialogue is crudely handled. Accused of being a bad husband, he bursts out laughing and says he doesn't like being bored. "We men are all the same, Countess. And she's always up to her neck in domesticity you know—children, school, and so forth. She doesn't complain." Then Vronsky appears. We are told at once of his chin, dark blue though freshly shaved; his strong teeth; his head nearly bald but beautifully shaped, with dark curls on the nape. He and Stiva arrange to dine the next day. He keeps looking towards the door. . . .

From *Tolstoy and the Novel*. © 1966 by John Bayley. Chatto & Windus, 1966.

They were certainly an odd pair. He was pallid, wrinkled, dried up. She had a low forehead, a short, almost retroussé nose, and was far too plump—a little more and she would have seemed monstrous. Indeed, without the great black eyelashes which made her grey eyes wonderful, the black curls on her forehead, a vigorous grace of movement like her brother's, and small feet and hands, she would have been downright ugly.

So these are the Karenins! If Tolstoy had retained the passage, even in a modified form, could we ever have got over the shock? We should have seen this little Renoir figure, this plump kitten, for the rest of the novel. She, Vronsky and Karenin would have been like the other fascinating but rather grotesque denizens of the high social jungle. It is a remarkable instance of the crudity of Tolstoy's initial externalisations. It has the vitality of Thackeray or Pisemsky but is certainly no better.

And in spite of the Pushkinian opening sentence Tolstoy has already ruptured the spell of Pushkinian narrative. That depends on a remarkable blend of simplicity and economy *without* externalisation. Unlike Merimée and eighteenth-century prose narrative, which it in some ways resembles, it is both bare and warm. Pushkin's complete, but as it were wordless, sympathy makes us intimate with his characters without his describing them. Tolstoy must describe: he positively itches to; but this early draft shows how important it is that he should first let us inside his main characters. It is all very well for these inhabitants of the haut monde, for a Kuragin, even for a Karenin, to be for us what they first look like; but for the vital persons it is different. Tolstoy expresses this difference in a comment in the completed novel about Anna. "Her charm lay precisely in the fact that her personality always stood out from her dress, that her dress was never conspicuous on her." If for "dress" here we read "outward appearance" we see that Tolstoy knows very well what has to be done. But of course a total personality can be treated by a novelist as Tolstoy in the first draft treats externals. Flaubert may not have known the colour of Emma's eyes, but he leaves us in no doubt that he knows everything about her personality. He shows us round it much as Tolstoy shows us round the salon in this first sketch. So does Proust with his characters. We do not forget that we are being shown something, and that this is the point of the exercise, and hence our growing gloom as the demonstration of Emma goes meticulously on. But with Tolstoy, personality has to stand out from description and dissection as Anna's stood out from her dress.

How is this to be done? In the first sketch Tolstoy made Anna a *jolie laide*, attractive to men in spite of being too plump and not pretty. In a second he tries another tack. Tatiana Sergeyevna (as she is now called) wears a yellow dress trimmed with black lace, more décolletée than any other in the room, and there is a provocative contrast between this costume and the simple sweetness of her beautiful skin, eyes and face. Again the likeness to her brother is noted, rather more emphatically. It is surely this likeness that gave Tolstoy the clue to his eventual process? Anna must not be introduced until we are entirely familiar with her brother: it is through him that we may first perceive and understand her. The peculiar advantage for Tolstoy of leading off with Stiva Oblonsky is that his nature, and the predicament in which it has placed him, require no preamble or filling in of background. In a flash we know what he is, and like all his friends and colleagues—even the Tartar waiter who brings him oysters—we stand and regard him with smiling indulgence. His physical charm affects people like something solid. Tolstoy makes us virtually of one flesh with him—it is as if we ourselves were waking up on the morocco couch in the dressing-room after a delightful dream—so like those in *War and Peace*, so unlike the terrible dream his sister will have at the end of the book.

> There was a dinner party in Darmstadt—no, not in Darmstadt but somewhere in America. Oh yes, Darmstadt was in America, and Alabin was giving the party. The dinner was served on glass tables, yes, and the tables sang *Il mio tesoro* . . . no, not exactly *Il mio tesoro*, but something better than that. And then there were some kind of little decanters that were really women.

With him we suddenly recall the terrible fuss the night before, when Dolly found out about the governess, and "there happened what happens to most people when unexpectedly caught in some shameful act." He had no time to assume the expression suitable to the position he was in and "involuntarily (reflex action of the brain, thought Oblonsky, who was fond of physiology) he smiled his usual kindly and therefore silly smile."

When he first hit on the idea of opening with Stiva, Tolstoy presented him at a cattle-show in a Moscow park, where Ordyntsev (Levin), "an agricultural expert, gymnast, and athlete," with "a Russian face," is showing some of his stock. The two were to welcome one another and talk about Kitty. The final version, showing Stiva waking up, dressing and going to the office, came later; and later still the opening epigram about happy and unhappy families. The strength of the first chapter is that it presents a man ideally suited to the scenic method, and who gives that method an absolute initial justification and authority which will never falter throughout the book. Not the least of Stiva's functions is to make us feel that we know everyone, and that everything about them is quite clear. Particularly everything about his sister.

Another role of Stiva's is no less important. It is to identify us, at the outset, as if it were in play, with the situation of an adulterer. The immediate and involuntary sympathy that we feel with him — perhaps identification rather than sympathy, for it is something physical rather than moral — will stay with us in all such situations throughout the book. It makes us realise, too, that what to one person (a participant, not a spectator) is merely unfortunate and a bore, can to others be deadly. Not only is nothing permanent in the world of *Anna Karenina* — nothing is seen in the same way by any two people. Anna cannot regard her brother's disgrace with the same disgust and misery as Dolly, not because she has an instinctive sympathy with it but because she is seeing it from a different angle. Anna herself will be subject to the sympathy of Dolly and Kitty at the end of the book, when just before her suicide they remark to one another how attractive she is, and yet how pathetic. The solitude of the point of view is unobtrusive, frightening, sublime. With Stiva, Tolstoy raises to its highest art his practice of letting the individual appear in the light of his own point of view. Though his sex life is presumably more complicated and sordid than that of any other character, it seems innocent to us because it seems so to him. Like an Elizabethan shepherd he gives a ballet girl a coral necklace, "and contrived, in the midday darkness of the theatre, to kiss her pretty face." More we do not see.

The scenic role of Stiva answers the criticism made, among others, by Percy Lubbock in *The Craft of Fiction* and by Arnold Bennett. For the former it is the presentation of Anna that is the chief flaw in the book, "a flaw which Tolstoy could not have avoided if he was determined to hold to his scenic plan." But, as we have seen [elsewhere], Tolstoy has a horror of backgrounds: they smell not only of "the novel" but of what I have tried to suggest by using the term "pastoral." However much Tolstoy may intervene and take charge in his own person, he never tries to take charge of a character's past life.

In *War and Peace* and *Anna Karenina* there are no exceptions to this. Tolstoy seems instinctively to feel that a character's past life is a kind of reality, a reality which the author has no right to possess himself of. A novelist should not have it both ways, owning both past and present: Tolstoy confines himself to what he can make of a character from the moment he creates him. It takes a Tolstoy to do this, but as a method it is surely self-justifying? Dostoevsky's method, oddly enough, is not dissimilar, though it is a dramatic and not a scenic method, and his references to the past ("that was before we knew what had taken place when X was at Y," etc.) are not intended to fill out a character but to contribute to the general dramatic atmosphere. There is a sense, indeed, in which both novelists resemble Shakespeare here: all three giants can afford to ignore the lesser writer's necessary claim to every sort of access to character and motive. Shakespeare's characters . . . are so full of life that they appear to have a past and a future which are no part of their creator's intention or requirement. So have Tolstoy's.

"The method of the book," writes Percy Lubbock, "does not arise out of the subject: in treating it Tolstoy simply used the method that was congenial to him without regarding the story that he had to tell." It is quite true that in starting so much with the idea of the novel, and using one of the oldest plots in the game, Tolstoy lays himself open. Granted the premise of *The Craft of Fiction*, Percy Lubbock's criticism is cogent enough, though it reminds us of eighteenth-century objections to Shakespeare's violation of dramatic rules.

> He began it as though Anna's break with the past was the climax to which her story was to mount, whereas it is really the point from which her story sets out for its true climax in her final catastrophe. And so the first part of the book is neither one thing nor another. . . . Tolstoy did not see how much more was needed than a simple personal impression of Anna, in view of all that is to come. Not she only, but her world, the world as she sees it, the past as it affects her — this too is demanded and for this he makes no provision. It is never really shown how she was placed in her life and what it meant to her: and the flare of passion has consequently no importance, no fateful bigness.

"To the very end," he sums up, "Anna is a wonderful woman whose early history has never been fully explained."

But even on the ground of technique the critic has chosen, this is not quite true. What is Stiva for? His past we know as instinctively as his present. We have also the Princess Barbara, Anna and Stiva's aunt, and she too — though the most minor of characters — is instantly visible and comprehensible. Dolly, "who knew she had been all her life a hanger-on of rich relatives," dislikes her, and is shocked to find her staying with Anna when Vronsky is "a perfect stranger to her." Her presence suggests the sort of background which Anna had known well when young. Tolstoy's worldliness is absolutely comprehensive, with the confidence that suggests an understanding all the more complete for being tacit. (It is very different from Proust's.) Clearly the Oblonsky family, a little like the Kuragins in *War and Peace*, although of the very highest society (it is the first thing Vronsky notes in Anna) did not have the sound and solid traditions taken for granted in the Rostov, Levin and Shcherbatsky families. They lived by wit rather than by custom. We can see Stiva living like this all through the book up to the moment when—his sister dead—he sends a triumphant if belated message to Dolly that he has managed to get the lucrative appointment to some board of directors. Equally clearly, the Vronsky family resembled the Oblonsky's rather than the others. Vronsky's mother is a splendidly and chillingly accurate portrait—a woman of the world with the cold good sense to see that affairs are all very well but that this kind of passion may ruin her son. Nothing is more revealing than the impression we get of her feelings about Anna after their night train journey together, when Vronsky meets his mother at the station. She likes Anna, but instantly grasps her status as a threat, not—as she herself has been—as a woman who likes affairs, but as a woman who unknowingly believes in passion.

Stiva married into a sound and stable family, and it is his salvation. However much he may deceive and impoverish Dolly he is secure because of her; nor does he fully realise how much his unchanging status and popularity owe to the stability of his family relations. His sister was much less lucky. She has no more natural talent for homemaking than her brother, no doubt because in the family there was no instinctively learnt tradition of home. Clearly that family found her a good match—rather a dull man, but perfectly presentable, and destined for the highest office. No doubt Princess Barbara, and others of the family too perhaps, saw excellent opportunities of sponging and place-seeking. And Anna—warm, hopeful, impulsive, and ready to please—would be perfectly willing. Ambitious and able, Karenin is a man without background: Anna must make the home, which she can't do. Nor can she after she has gone off with Vronsky. Dolly spots at once that Anna is like a guest in her own house, just as she once spotted that the Karenin household was not really like a home, and that Anna made rather too much of her role as a mother. It is Vronsky who runs everything, gives a considering glance at the table, catches the butler's eye. Vronsky, we remember, has never known family life. Now he is self-consciously and rather pathetically playing at it, with no one to embody for him how it naturally and simply happens.

In an early draft the pair marry after Anna's divorce, and have two children. Interestingly, Vronsky was given in this version a much more stable family background; and for the same reason he was presented as genuinely in love with Kitty and about to propose to her. Tolstoy portrayed, too, his chagrin that his children by Anna cannot be brought up as he was—he has cut himself off from the roots that should have grown through him into a new generation family life based on the old. If Tolstoy had held to the plan of their remarriage the pair would have remained separated by their different family backgrounds, because they had sought to unite themselves solely by passion. With this as their visible and necessary tie, the background of neither could have helped them, and the discrepancy between the two would have eventually turned things bad.

Such things, it seems to me, are present and visible in the novel, and provide a history as we understand a history in life: not something simply told to us, that is, but to some extent found out and deduced for ourselves. If Tolstoy "did not see how much more was needed," may it not have been because he assumed the reader would provide it? He may have been wrong in assuming this, but it is one of his most mesmeric characteristics that he writes about Moscow and Petersburg social and family life as if it were a universal thing, and as if his readers would understand what he understood in it. Possibly Homer made the same assumptions. Certainly Balzac and Proust did not. They are showing us over their acquired territories: Tolstoy belongs to his. If Balzac had been a banker he would not have wanted to explain to us all the processes of banking; if Proust had been a duke it would not have occurred to him to conduct us with such relish through all the tones and nuances of the French aristocracy. In Tolstoy's hands Moscow and Petersburg family life becomes a universal thing. Irrespective of social level some families are like this, some like that: and the conventions of collective existence in each powerfully affect the fates and fortunes of individual members, when these go on to lead their own lives. Jane Austen, like Tolstoy, took this for granted. In *Mansfield Park* she shows us nothing of the Crawfords' upbringing, but she makes quite clear what effect its shortcomings had on the crucial decisions of their adult lives.

If the Rostovs are such a solid family, it may be objected, what about Natasha's signal lapse from virtue? Yet Natasha was a girl, and behaved as any spirited girl might have done—the impress of family backbone appears later in life. If Pierre had turned out as unintimate and unattentive as Karenin, Natasha would not have been likely to go off with another man. "Principle" shows itself not in the way you make your bed but in how you lie on it. But in a sense all this is by the way. Anna is of course not the product of a bad or broken home. In suggesting how much we may be said to know about her early history I wished only to show that the accusation of a gap, a Tolstoyan hiatus, is not really justified. The real significance of our impression of a gap, though, lies in the fact that Anna comes to feel it herself.

She cannot review and consider her life calmly—*therefore we must not.* She does not know herself what she has done or will do; she does not know "how she is placed in her life and what it means to her"; she takes it for granted until the crisis comes, and after that she cannot reconstitute it. This is part temperament, part upbringing. She has her brother's power of living in the moment. If we knew about her previous life we should know (as of course Tolstoy knows) what she might do. She must be continuously immediate, terribly and exhilaratingly so. And so successful is Tolstoy here that we feel that most other comparable heroines in fiction are in some curious way *safe*. Poor Eugénie Grandet, poor Emma Bovary and Isabel Archer and Lily Dale! —but the reader cannot quite escape the impression that they have nothing to worry about. They are so snugly placed in their novels. Indeed many persons in life, too, seem placed there like these characters in novels, and can, as it were, present their past and future in the midst of their present experience, but not Anna. If the Crawfords may be a minor English analogue for Anna's family side, the only one for the immediate *apparition* of her is Catherine in *Wuthering Heights*.

And perhaps Shakespeare's Cressida. Both have a presentness, a momentariness, about them that can be shocking and unnerving. "Anna, is this you?" asks Karenin, echoing Shakespeare's Troilus—"This is, and is not, Cressid"—as he echoes any amount of shocked and anonymous incredulity in real life. Tolstoy brings home to us the seriocomic way in which we do keep other people in our everyday consciousness by feeling them to be fixed in life as if in a book. We assume that they will continue to do what we are accustomed to them doing, as we assume that Pip has great expectations, and that King Lear will always divide his kingdom between his three daughters. Living, in fact, depends on this process.

> Karenin was being confronted with life—with the possibility of his wife's loving somebody else, and this seemed stupid and incomprehensible to him, because it was life itself. He had lived and worked all his days in official spheres, which deal with reflections of life, and every time he had knocked up against life itself he had stepped out of its way. He now experienced a sensation such as a man might feel who, while quietly crossing a bridge over an abyss, suddenly sees that the bridge is falling to pieces and that he is facing the abyss. The abyss was real life; the bridge was the artificial life Karenin had been living.

It is a good example of Tolstoy's closeness to the reactions of his characters. Whether or not in his daily routine he has been "living" is neither here nor there. The important thing is that he is now confronted with a terrible and unexpected situation which he instantly feels to be "real life." He is as unaccustomed as most people to "putting himself in thought and feeling into another being." (In Dolly's daydream of taking a lover, she imagines with relish the amazement and incomprehension of Stiva, who takes her as much for granted as Karenin takes Anna.)

Anna is in a similar state: she is amazed at her own reactions, her new-found impenetrability and refusal to be understood. We can no more "see" her than Karenin can. Coming back from the party where she has met Vronsky again (the same party that figures in the two possible opening drafts), "her face shone with a vivid glow, but not a joyous glow—it resembled the terrible glow of a conflagration on a dark night." This is one of Tolstoy's best similes, and it shows us how right he was not to retain those first physical impressions of Anna—embonpoint, shoulders, air of jolie laide, etc. The more she is in love the less she is visible, to us and to the other characters.

She begins to be a centre of isolation and unreality. So she becomes for Kitty, who admired her so much and imagined her at the ball in a lilac dress. But she appeared in black, which at once seemed right, and now her shoulders and hair can be described (though it is not her but a Madame Korsunova who is the most décolletée woman present) and there is something brilliant and pitiless about her. Kitty cannot talk to her any more, nor she to Kitty. The hand on Vronsky's shoulder is not the "small energetic hand" which had comforted Dolly. In the morning the children had adored her, but the next day they seem to have forgotten their new aunt and are quite indifferent about her.

Again Stiva acts as a kind of index to her. When Vronsky first meets her he smiles involuntarily at her charm, as everyone smiles at Stiva. They will always go on smiling at Stiva but Anna has become different, and at the ball Vronsky has a submissive, doglike look. Her whole being now seems indeterminate, like fire or water: the stability of others, Stiva, Karenin, her maid Annushka ("dozing, her broad hands, with a hole in one of the gloves, holding the red bag on her lap") enable us to perceive and inhabit the strange element. Returning to the country after his failure with Kitty, Levin cheers up and reflects that "he was himself and did not wish to be anyone else." It is the great Tolstoyan resource and comfort, the *samodovolnost* of *War and Peace*, but with Anna it has quite disintegrated. "Am I myself, or another?" she wonders in the train. The train, the storm, the shrieking snow, whirl her away from her pleasure in her travelling arrangements, the pillow from the little red bag, the paper knife, the English novel.

> Anna read and understood, but it was unpleasant to read, that is to say, to follow the reflection of other people's lives. She was

too eager to live herself. When she read how the heroine of the novel nursed a sick man, she wanted to move about the sick-room with noiseless footsteps; when she read of a member of Parliament making a speech, she wished to make that speech; when she read how Lady Mary rode to hounds, teased her sister-in-law, and astonished everybody by her boldness — she wanted to do it herself. But there was nothing to be done, so she forced herself to read, while her little hand toyed with the smooth paper-knife.

The ball, the storm, and Anna's return to Petersburg, are breathtaking in their assurance. Metaphor, insight, and the objectification of a state with which he was himself becoming more and more familiar — they were never combined more felicitously in his art. And all these climactic scenes are shot through with humour. Anna may have been triumphant and pitiless at the ball, but as she reads her English novel, or notices her husband's ears on Petersburg station, she is touching and comic. Yet the climax of the seduction is the end of life flowing like a fountain or blazing like a fire: it is like the constriction of the black bag, the confrontation of death. Everything shrinks to one fact.

> "It's all over," she said. "I have nothing but you left. Remember that."

The despair of the discovery remains with her to the end, however great her subsequent joy, possessiveness and pleasure. She compared herself to a starving man given food, and we remember this when Levin is compared to a starving man in a toyshop. Yet Tolstoy's fear of sex, as of death, does not obtrude: the discovery of what they have done is the lovers' alone, and we completely accept that what Tolstoy tells us is their own reaction.

What does obtrude a little are Tolstoy's novelish devices. The storm, the journey, and the meeting with Vronsky and then Karenin, are no more like a novel than the English novel Anna reads on the train resembles *Anna Karenina*. They are an onrush of life and power. Not so the omens — the man killed on the line as Anna arrives in Moscow — or the schematisation of "the peacemakers." Admirably done as is Anna's intervention with Dolly on her brother's behalf, Tolstoy is surely pulling the wires when Anna urges Dolly to remember that men, however disgustingly they may behave with actresses and governesses, never lose their reverence for The Home. Nor does it seem other than contrived that when he meets Anna again in Petersburg Vronsky should have been engaged on rescuing two comrades from a farcical situation. "Blessed are the peacemakers, for they shall be saved," said Princess

Betsy, remembering she had heard someone say something like that. The humour is engaging, but the atmosphere of biblical quotations seems to close in on us—"He saved others" and "Vengeance is mine: I will repay." It is left to Stiva to appear wholly himself in the beneficent role, and that because he might do as much damage as he does good. At his dinner party he seems strangely like the hero of the novel, getting Levin and Kitty engaged at last as simply as he gratifies Karenin and "kneads all that society dough till the drawing-room was in first-rate form."

Almost any party demonstrates an aspect of Tolstoy's Law—his clear stream of narration and comment always seems more full of meaning than his deliberate effects, however just and masterly these may be. Kitty struggling with a pickled mushroom as she asks Levin if there are bears on his estate, and the same Kitty after marriage tidying up the dying Nicholas and making him comfortable; Turovtsin, who helped Dolly when her children had scarlet fever, laughing so much that the thick end of his asparagus falls in the butter sauce; Stiva laying his hand for a moment on the hotel waiter's head—these facts seem more meaningful, as well as more vital, than the metaphoric pattern, the omens, and the peacemaking parallels.

More meaningful, too, than the wider parallel between Levin's ideas and convictions and the multifarious action of the novel which invisibly and silently corroborates them. In *War and Peace* there seems no predetermined connection between events and Tolstoy's views about them. Event and view only finally coincide in the triumph of the marriage sequence at the close. In *Anna Karenina* their coincidence is already implied at the beginning. When we are informed that Levin thought of family life as the the thing that really mattered, and imagined the family scene in his home before he imagined the woman who would share it with him, we feel that—through him—conception and view is anticipating character and actuality. Levin should expand and not contract the scope of the book. On the whole he does, and so earns his decisive role: the shooting, the mowing, the wedding, the elections, are all excellent, assimilated into the flow and yet far enough from the tragedy to relieve us from it, and contrast truly with it. Nonetheless it is the function of Levin as unconscious arbiter, in whose attitude solutions are already present in schematic form, that is a more serious danger to the scope of the novel than is Tolstoy's use of the scenic method. In spite of its omissions that method enlarges and expands, and nothing that expands can go wrong in Tolstoy— the longer he goes on and the more he gets in the better. It is contraction and symbolic schematisation that are the dangers.

But we can become aware of these as much through the original participants of the novel as through Levin. Pivotal episode as it is, in that it precipitates Anna's confession to her husband, the steeplechase at Krasnoe Selo is not quite the self-justified thing we should expect, when we consider the status of other such great scenes in Tolstoy, like the two hunts in *War and Peace* and the two shooting-parties in *Anna*. The trouble seems to be that Tolstoy tried to make it too symbolically decisive, too eloquent of the relations between Anna and Vronsky. Literal genius as he is, Tolstoy's symbolic touch is far from delicate, far from being the sort of poetically instinctive thing that it can be in Turgenev at his best, or in novelists otherwise as dissimilar as Hardy and D. H. Lawrence. Dr F. R. Leavis has indeed compared the scene unfavourably with episodes in Lawrence's novels, concluding that while the latter have an instinctive psychological relevance to the author's intention, Tolstoy is easily seduced from the current of his novel by anything fashionable, of the beau monde.

So much the better for Tolstoy, given the kind of writer he is, and would that it were so here. Lawrence's imagination can be reserved to him: it does not make a good stick to beat Tolstoy. Tolstoy himself said that he had no imagination, and his enormous literalness does seem to leave our ordinary use of the word standing. Not for him the almost unconscious creation of symbolic atmosphere that we associate with a vivid literary imagination. The railway and the storm in *Anna* is only a partial exception. The suicide of a despairing woman under a train was the occurrence from which the novel began; making the lovers' first meeting in a railway station was a logical step which would be equally effective in any other writer—it is not specifically Tolstoyan. The linkages by means of metaphor are almost a substitute for the symbolic imagination, as if Tolstoy felt that a novel—"the first I have attempted"—required something of the sort. They are inherently clumsy, like the Dickensian touches he sometimes falls back on when a scene is antipathetic to him, or an individual physically unattractive—the divorce lawyer who catches moths, or Karenin's habit of cracking his finger-joints. These are neither imaginative nor literal.

The early drafts leave us in no doubt that Tolstoy intended a symbolic parallel between the fate of Anna and of Vronsky's mare in the steeplechase. Indeed both have the same name—Tania. In the final version the parallel is no longer emphasised, but it is still there, and it collides in an agreeably but unintentionally comic way with the superb literalness with which Tolstoy describes the mare and her trainer.

> Frou-Frou was of medium size and by no means free from blemish. She was slenderly built. Her chest, though well arched, was narrow. Her hindquarters tapered rather too much, and her legs,

especially her hind legs, were perceptibly bowed inwards. Neither fore nor hind legs were particularly muscular, but on the other hand she was exceptionally broad in the girth, now that she was lean from her strict training. She appeared all the more narrow in build because so deep in the breadth. But she possessed in the highest degree a characteristic that made one forget all her defects. This was her thoroughbred quality — the kind of blood that *tells*, as they say in English. The muscles, clearly marked beneath the network of sinews stretched in the fine mobile skin as smooth as satin, seemed hard as bone. Her lean head with the prominent bright and sparkling eyes, broadened out to her muzzle with its wide crimson nostrils. Her whole appearance, particularly about the head, was spirited and yet gentle. . . .

As soon as Vronsky entered she took a deep breath, and turning her prominent eyes so that the whites became bloodshot, looked from the other side of the box at the newcomers, shook her muzzle, and stepped lightly from foot to foot.

"See how nervous she is," said the Englishman.

"You darling!" said Vronsky, going up to the horse and soothing her.

But the nearer he came the more nervous she grew. Only when he reached her head did she suddenly calm down, and the muscles under her fine and delicate coat vibrated. Vronsky stroked her firm neck, adjusted a lock of her hair that had got on the wrong side of her sharply-defined withers, and brought his face close to her dilated nostrils, delicate as a bat's wing. Her extended nostrils loudly inhaled and exhaled her breath; she set back one of her finely pointed ears with a start and stretched out her black firm lips towards Vronsky, as if wishing to catch hold of his sleeve. But remembering her muzzle she jerked it, and again began stepping from one of her finely chiselled feet to the other.

This is, as Chaucer would say, the most *horsely* of horses. It is a superlative instance of the power of Tolstoy's creations to be "the thing they are and not another thing." And it shows us why Anna and the mare cannot be metaphorically related. The early versions present an elementary but effective dramatic relation which Tolstoy entirely removed in the final text, while involuntarily retaining the ghost of the old identification. His first idea was that Tania the heroine should be virtually responsible for the disaster which overtakes her namesake the mare and Balachev (as Vronsky was first called).

She is determined to watch the race, but she has had a terrible dream about her lover's fall at the main obstacle, and therefore she stands with a friend beside the smaller jump at the end of the course. Balachev sees her as he approaches and it unnerves him. His jump is a little premature, and in an elaborate passage Tolstoy describes—more convincingly than in the few oddly perfunctory words of the final version—how the mare slips on a broken turf as she lands, tries to change feet and recover herself, but falls heavily, breaking her spine. Tania runs up and asks Balachev if he is hurt. He limps off without replying.

The symbolic significance is graphic and clear. Tania has helped to lose Balachev the race: she will now ruin his life and that of her husband, and destroy herself when he sees what havoc she has caused. The relation of heroine to horse does not matter, because both are so closely involved with the rider in the drama of his fall. The final version is not so graphic, but it is far more effective psychologically. It is in keeping with the tone of personal relations throughout the book, for instead of bringing the lovers together it emphasises their isolation from each other. The point (implicit in the fine description) is that—so far from there being any resemblance—Frou-Frou and her fate belong to a different world from Anna and hers. In the excitement of the race Vronsky has entirely forgotten about Anna, a kind of forgetting which in the later stages of their relationship will call forth her most demonic jealousy. Vronsky's failure and disappointment are wholly his own: Anna's anxiety and relief are wholly hers. Tolstoy conveys their separation in the mere account of Frou-Frou and her trainer, and in Vronsky's preoccupation with his horse and his rival, but he also underlines it by a simple narrative device. He describes the race twice: first as Vronsky rode it, and then from the point of view of Anna and Karenin as spectators. Such drama as remains is now not between the lovers but between the wife and the husband, who observes her terror at the news of Vronsky's fall and her indifference to that of the others.

Through the early versions Vronsky evolves always in the direction of greater self-possession, of tranquil uncommitted aplomb. He evolves, in fact, to become *incapable of a dramatic relationship*. The early Vronskys are passionate and vulnerable, as capable—significantly—of a dramatic and sympathetic relation with Karenin himself as with Anna. Their dramatic potential shows even in their appearance—young Balachev, as well as being bald and blue-chinned, wears a single silver earring: it is an old family custom. One cannot imagine our Vronsky doing anything so outré. Balachev-Vronsky is not unlike Mitya in *The Brothers Karamazov*—his passion has the same directness and unintimate animal facility. The dramatic triangle of the steeplechase is repeated in that between himself, Anna and Karenin. But in the final Vronsky, Tolstoy has returned to something much more than a subtle and intimate version of "the superfluous man."

The advantage of this Vronsky, in terms of a high challenge to the author, is that he is the last person apparently to go overboard in the way he does. The passion of Balachev-Vronsky for Anna is just what we would have expected, and any interest it had would be collective and dramatic rather than intimate and psychological. But as novel readers rather than dramatic participants we are, so to speak, much more like the final Vronsky than the earlier one, and more ready to enter fully into his motives and feelings. Tolstoy makes us feel that if *we* were to go overboard with Anna we should do it like this, that we should be as adroit, as collected, only realising after each step had been taken how deeply we had committed ourselves. It is because we are so close to him when he has his moments of stocktaking, sitting down in a clean shirt the morning after the steeplechase to square up his debts and consider his relations with Anna, that we still feel close at the climax of his humiliation with Karenin when Anna is so ill, and even in his attempt at suicide. Tolstoy's secret here is to compel a naturally undramatic character to participate in drama against his will. Instead of being the natural outcome of character and the climax of Anna's situation, illness and Vronsky's suicide attempt is unexpected and without a sequel, for (Tolstoy implies) it has no lasting significance for the personalities involved and for daily life as they have to go on living it.

The final Vronsky has no self-destructive impulse. His samodovolnost has about it an alert and instinctive decorum which makes him liked and admired: and he is not adroitly calculating—indeed he fails to calculate in his military life the results of having turned down an important post. He assumed his lack of vulgar zeal would commend itself, and was chagrined to find himself misunderstood: instead of respecting in him the higher self-seeking, his superiors assumed he was not interested, and were quite prepared to leave him to go his own way. He meets Anna at the moment when his role of disinterest has begun to pall.

Tolstoy the analyst could not have described a love affair without an element of calculation in it—that is why the dramatic spontaneity of the early Vronsky-Balachev had to undergo modification. There is nothing repellent in the calculation; it is simply human and does not make Vronsky unsympathetic, but it indicates why he would be more successful in the role of lover than in that of husband. He wants to do everything properly, but he supposes that doing things properly in love requires the jockey's, the general's or the gambler's powers of skill and concentration. Although he does not

confide in them, he feels that the only two of his friends who would understand him are the gambler Yashvin, and the successful commander Serpukhov-
skoy. Both would grasp the seriousness of the business, the *intentness*, and
would realise from their own philosophy that this is his way of fulfilling
himself, or risking everything.

But when he is left alone with Anna he finds there is nothing left for
this power of intentness to accomplish. He had been flattered that Serpukhov-
skoy thought him a necessary man, but now he has become a superfluous
one, whose only function is to continue to tell Anna that he loves her. In
the end he grimaces with pain at the very word "love," and at Anna's inces-
sant and bitter repetition of it. The careful and methodical side of him, to
which love—like power or war—had seemed to offer a high challenge, must
now devote itself to estate management and local politics, and even these
activities are poisoned by the aftermath of his coup de main. He hankers
for any ordinary occupation away from Anna. "The innocent mirth of the
elections, and this dismal burdensome love to which he must return, struck
Vronsky by their contrast. But he had to go, and he took the first train that
night for home."

Solipsism in *Anna* is as joyful as in *War and Peace*, as shiningly serene.
In the first half of the novel, at least, the solipsistic man is happy and therefore
right. But instead of being a part of the natural order of things, this rightness
conceals a strange irony. When Anna and Vronsky are happiest in their love
they are alone: we never see their happiness together, as we see that of the
married couples at the end of *War and Peace*. Vronsky is happiest on his own
when he is going to see Anna, not when he is with her.

> He put down his legs, threw one of them over the other, and
> placing his arm across it felt its firm calf, where he had hurt it
> in the fall the day before, and then, throwing himself back, sighed
> deeply several times.
>
> "Delightful! O delightful!" he thought. He had often before
> been joyfully conscious of his body, but had never loved himself,
> his own body, as he did now. It gave him pleasure to feel the
> slight pain in his strong leg, to be conscious of the muscles of
> his chest moving as he breathed. That clear, cool August day which
> made Anna feel so hopeless seemed exhilarating and invigorating
> to him and refreshed his face and neck, which were glowing after
> their washing and rubbing. The scent of brilliantine given off by
> his moustache seemed peculiarly pleasant in the fresh air. All that
> he saw from the carriage window through the cold pure air in
> the pale light of the evening sky seemed as fresh, bright and

vigorous as he was himself. The roofs of the houses glittered in the evening sun; the sharp outlines of the fences and corners of buildings, the figures of people and vehicles they occasionally met, the motionless verdure of the grass and trees, the fields of potatoes with their clear-cut ridges, the slanting shadows of the houses and trees, the bushes and even the potato ridges — it was all pleasant and like a landscape newly painted and varnished.

When he sees her, "a thrill passed like electricity through his body, and with renewed force he became conscious of himself, from the elastic movement of his firm legs to the motion of his lungs as he breathed, and of something tickling his lips."

Vronsky's self-sufficiency at this moment is outrageous, sublime; he can no more deny it than Stiva could prevent that stupid kindly smile ("reflex action of the brain") coming over his face at a most inopportune time. For the men in *Anna* it is the body that leads and the feelings that follow; the state of one's own body, not other people's feelings, tells one whether an experience is good or bad. For Vronsky, the sign and seal of love is this extraordinary increase in his samodovolnost. It is not Anna but *himself* who is aware of the joyful tickling of his moustache. Samodovolnost is a far more shameless thing in *Anna* than it was in *War and Peace*, and it seems likely that, even at its most apparently serene, there is now in it a sharp element of self-hatred. *Anna*, as Dostoevsky remarked, is by no means an innocent book. Tolstoy was well aware of the destructive potential of this joyful solipsism.

We already know how much Anna is irritated by Vronsky's calm happiness. The cold fresh summer day, so enchanting to him, is for her malignant and disintegrating. She wishes Vronsky to confer on her the same joyful unity that he feels himself, but she knows that he will not and cannot. How could there be unity between two persons in such entirely different *physical* states? She must tell him that her husband now knows.

> If at this news he would say to her, firmly and passionately, and without an insant's hesitation: "Give up everything and fly with me!" she would leave her son and go with him. But the news had not the effect on him that she had desired: he only looked as if he had been offended by something.

She thinks this cold severity is aimed at her, but it is only caused by his gravely satisfied contemplation of a duel with Karenin. Worst, of all, she realises that his reaction to the news is not spontaneous.

> She understood at once that he had already considered this by himself, knew that whatever he might say he would not tell her all that he was thinking, and that her last hopes had been deceived. This was not what she had expected.

Reactions in Tolstoy are not spontaneous—only physically involuntary. Like Stiva, Vronsky cannot keep a certain look off his face, the look with which he imagines himself confronting Karenin's pistol. Even his solicitude irritates her, for it is without intuition. He supposes that telling her husband was agonisingly difficult, but that, as she dryly tells him, came of itself. Yet this failure to meet each other is not insisted on: there is one deeply moving moment when sobs choke her as she says she is proud of his love, and "for the first time in his life Vronsky too felt ready to cry."

Anna goes back to Petersburg and another misunderstanding occurs. Karenin is fresh from his triumph at an important committee meeting, and the last thing he wants is a showdown. All he requires for the moment is that everything should remain outwardly the same, so that he can at least enjoy his political victory. Anna says timidly that their relations cannot be the same, and, too late, realises that her husband is not referring to their going to bed together, but only to the proprieties being observed. He rubs this in with hatred and sarcasm, and her humiliation is complete.

In the next chapter we are back with Levin and his ploughs and hayfields, and we begin to realise that his nature obeys the same laws as Vronsky's, and Stiva's. His spells of euphoria are perfectly his own, without relation to what is going on around him. When he is gloomy he feels the peasants misunderstand and dislike him; that they break his farm implements on purpose and have no wish for improvements of any kind. When he is cheerful he sees a wonderful future for his new system and ideas. He is feeling happy about his book when his brother Nicholas arrives, dying of consumption. At first he feels ashamed to remain happy when his brother is dying, but Nicholas reminds him of death as malignantly and incessantly as Anna will remind Vronsky of love, and with the same result. His brother at once attacks the ideas of his book, not because it is bad but because it is written by a man who will go on living, while he himself must die.

> "You do not want to establish anything. You simply want to be original, as you have always done, and to show that you are not just exploiting the peasants, but have ideas!"
>
> "You think so? Well then, leave me alone!" said Levin, and he felt that a muscle was uncontrollably quivering in his left cheek.

Life is telling death to leave it alone, as self-sufficiency will tell love to do so. But in the night Levin gets up, and looks in the glass at his teeth, his hair and his arms. "I am working; I want to do something, and I had forgotten it will all end in death."

I have remarked how Tolstoy's enormous vitality continually displayed itself in his way of narrating by two "positives," where one might have expected a positive and a negative. Thus Prince Andrew cannot find his former love for Natasha, but in its place is a new, sober and perturbing sort of tenderness; or Levin himself does not feel the expected love for his newborn child but rather a "new and distressing sense of fear," and "the consciousness of another vulnerable region." These are new and vital discoveries which will in turn give place to further discoveries. In *War and Peace* life and death are themselves such positives. Andrew seems to go from one to another as he does from one phase of experience to another. Death is described almost as a different aspect of life. But in *Anna* death appears as a true negation, which cannot be faced because it offers nothing imaginable to experience. And love itself is not very different.

Levin's period of euphoria, as he waits to engage himself officially to Kitty, is just as solipsistic as Vronsky's in the carriage on the way to Anna. But because his love is secret and self-created, Vronsky's happiness begins and ends in his own body, while Levin's joy is shared (as he thinks) with everyone he meets. His self-preoccupation has not only a public licence but the property of making others happy, as young Rostov's happiness infected the German innkeeper on whom he was billeted, as if both wanted to exclaim: "*Vivat die ganze Welt.*" The waiter at the hotel seems to respond to Levin's joy, "as men get infected by others' yawning." And Kitty's parents are infected too. "The old couple seemed to have become confused for the moment, and did not know whether it was they who were again in love or only their daughter." The idea of "infection" in this marvellous and moving passage seems to correspond closely to Tolstoy's formula of how we are "infected" by good art. The artist's joy in creation is solipsistic, but we share in it with him if what he describes is universal and necessary.

Levin's meeting with Kitty is attended by the same kind of misunderstandings and failures of communication as that of Anna and Vronsky, but they are completely swallowed up in the human and social necessity of their coming together. They are in love because it is necessary for them to be so in order to fulfil their lives. Both are convinced it was certain to happen, and Kitty thinks she is telling the truth when she says: "I always loved you only, but I was carried away." Natasha might have said the same to Pierre. Whatever she felt for Andrew or Kuragin, or Kitty for Vronsky, cannot afterwards be called love because it came to nothing. Even more unblushingly calm is the disclosure by Tolstoy that deep in Kitty's heart "was the fear and humiliation of being an old maid." Levin apprehends this, but instead of reflecting that this motive might be more important to her than his own personal charms, "he too felt the fear and humiliation." It infects him as his joy in the betrothal infected others. There is a touching irony in the fact that Levin loves Kitty more, through sensing that she does not love him so much as a person but as a means to an end; while Vronsky does not sense Anna's desperate hunger for him personally, but sees himself playing a role — that of the dignified lover facing the injured husband's fire. It is Vronsky's impossible task to embody love, while Levin has only to be its vessel and representative.

Anna has to keep the word love because it is all she has, a hard object to fling in Vronsky's teeth, until it becomes identified with the death she will also fling at him. The account of her consciousness in the carriage and train at the end is strinkingly similar in tone to those of Vronsky in his carriage and Levin's night before the betrothal. In order to kill time, Levin goes with Koznyshev to a Moscow town council meeting.

> What seemed remarkable to Levin was that they were all perfectly transparent to him that day, and that by means of little signs which he had never noticed before he recognised the soul of each, and clearly saw they were all kind, and — in particular — were all extremely fond of him.

Anna has the opposite experience. From the depths of her despair she can see equally clearly that they are all vile. "That man wants to astonish everybody and is very well satisfied with himself." She knows that Vronsky will not be unfaithful to her, or go off with the young Princess Sorokina, but this makes no difference. She sees that Vronsky wants to relax, to be kind and familial, but for her that would be hell, "for where love ceases, there hate begins." She realises her compulsive need to make Vronsky suffer for the suffering he has caused her.

Tolstoy accepts with his usual calm the human urge to repay in kind. After his rejection, Levin was ashamed to find how agreeable it was to hear that Kitty was ill "and was suffering — she who had made him suffer so much." Anna's impulse is the same as that of her persecutors. Karenin "does not acknowledge it to himself," but he wishes her to suffer, and under the influence of religion and Lydia Ivanovna he can make this desire respectable. Lydia Ivanovna herself, who claims that she can "understand immorality but not cruelty," achieves her own purpose in her reply to Anna's request to see her son, the purpose "which she had hidden even from herself." "Her letter wounded Anna to the depths of her soul."

Vengeance is one of Tolstoy's fictional themes, but he does not overdo it. He does not forget that most human beings are incapable of feeling one thing for long, even the desire to get their own back. He makes us realise how dependent most novelists are on the obsessiveness, or at least the unusual single-mindedness, of their characters. He makes us wonder whether George Eliot's Tito Melema and Rosamond Vincy, or Henry James's Gilbert Osmond, would have been *quite* so unremitting in their selfishness or their vindictiveness. The impulse to please, to make up for things, to provoke confidence and gratitude, simply to tease or be teased — even the selfish and the vindictive must feel this at times. And Anna's nature is not selfish or vindictive. The most touching thing on her last drive is when she sees an absurd name — Tyutkin — over a hairdresser's shop. "*Je me fais coiffer par Tyutkin* — I shall tell him that when he comes back she thought, and smiled." But then she remembers she has no one now to share something funny with. The touch both emphasises the imminence of catastrophe and deprives it of inevitability. They might have made a go of it. Anna might have acquiesced in Vronsky's diminished passion; her "demons" would always have come back, but there is much in life she enjoys and could go on enjoying, and she recognises this up to the last moment.

What crushes Anna most at the end is not, in fact, her sense of the impossibility of life with Vronsky, but her sense of isolation. And the chilling thing is how completely and how casually Dolly and Kitty, who are genuinely attached to her, have come to accept that isolation. It is her sense of being outcast from the kind of society in which she is most naturally at home, and where at the beginning of the book she was at home, that gives Anna her final despair. When Anna leaves them at the end, Kitty and Dolly — as they pass on to their preoccupations — remark how charming she is.

> "But there is something pathetic about her, terribly pathetic."
> "Yes, but today there is something peculiar about her," said Dolly. "When I was seeing her out, there in the hall, I thought she was going to cry."

It is the tone of this exchange which is most final. Ordinary society has not so much excluded Anna as simply failed to see how much she needs it. She has become accepted as being a different sort of person, and to her this is the final loneliness.

Yet Tolstoy does not attempt to convince us that isolation is the human fate, or that love as Anna and Vronsky experience it is necessarily a matter

of isolation and misunderstanding. At no point, either, are we asked to accept anything definitive about passion, nor are the numerous contrasting patterns of love required to imply a judgment on the central one. Levin, Kitty
and Dolly may sometimes appear as ideal figures, full of the unsought wisdom
of the ages, but they are disposed—as it were helplessly—among others, of
their kind, who are the same and yet different. There is Stiva; Koznyshev
and Varenka, disappointed and yet relieved after their failure to get engaged
in the mushroom wood; the egregious Sappho Stolz and Liza Merkalova,
as assertively alive as the main characters, and living endorsements of Princess
Betsy's dictum—"You see, a thing may be looked at tragically and turned
to a torment, or looked at quite simply, even gaily."

The sensations lead and the emotions follow. The difficulty of coming
to any conclusions about life is that the body does not remain in the same
state for long enough. When Anna is ill she feels love and admiration for
her husband, as if her dream of having two husbands who both loved her
had come true: when she recovers he excites in her only repulsion and fear.
And Karenin himself recovers from the forgiveness, the dignity, and the
simplicity which the strain of her illness had produced in him. Rage, sorrow, confession, repentance are almost equally gratifying and cathartic to
the body, like sneezing, sweating or shedding tears. Before the climax Karenin
goes to Anna carrying his rage like a cup he is anxious not to spill; when
she is ill he prays that the pleasure of forgiving may not be taken from him,
and he feels "a sense of joy at the greatness of his own humility." When
he is gloomily contemplating Anna's newly born daughter "suddenly a smile,
wrinkling the skin on his forehead and making his hair move, came out on
his face."

Vronsky's move to shoot himself is like a gesture of physical exaspera-
tion. "With a strong movement of his whole hand, as if to clench his fist,
he pulled the trigger." The attempt at suicide made in that gesture is caused
by the torture of his humiliation. He and Karenin have changed roles. It
is himself, and not the deceived husband, who turns out to be ridiculous.
Powerful emotions—hate, love, forgiveness—are not only good to feel in
themselves, they confer dignity on the person who feels them. For Tolstoy—so
unlike Dostoyevski here—shame and humiliation do not. For both Vronsky
and Levin it is not the best and the worst things in their lives that they
remember but the moments of stupidity, awkwardness. "Most terrible of
all was the ridiculous and shameful figure he had cut. . . . 'Take away his
hands,' Anna's voice is saying. Karenin pulls away his hands, and he is conscious of the shame-suffused and stupid expression of his own face."

But for Vronsky, too, the anguish does not last. He and Anna both recover; they meet again; they are as they were before, and so is Karenin. So exultant, so exhaustive is the narrative that we have no feeling of anticlimax, no impression of pointlessness; nor do we feel that Tolstoy has wished to make some point. He never suggests *himself* that strong emotion is physical in its origin, and therefore ephemeral, and in a sense without moral significance; that Vronsky, Anna and Karenin feel so differently about each other and their situation when in a heightened physical state, but that they are returned unchanged to the "coarse power" of habitual personal and social need. It is we who receive this impression amongst others, not he who appears to give it. We cannot draw any conclusions about the trio from their behaviour here, nor make any generalised deductions from it about human nature. It is a good example of the indirection of Tolstoy's grasp, and his power of imitating the deceptiveness of life itself, making his whole picture — like that of Mikhaylov when his guests are studying it — "come alive with the inexpressible complexity of everything that lives."

Formal ideas about our emotional states — like the James-Lange theory of their identification with their physical expression, or the rather similar theories of Sartre — cannot, of course, suggest life in this way. Indeed Sartre's fictional exemplifications of his theory remain precisely that: by maintaining his ideas his characters forfeit the possibility of total life. Life deceives as Tolstoy does: it suggests explanations only to contradict them, unintentionally as it seems. Few persons were more spontaneous in their affections, more rooted in their devotion, than the Countess Rostov. Yet we found her at the end of her life putting aside the miniature of the dead Count which Pierre has brought her, because she did not want to feel grief at that moment — the moment in her daily routine when she was accustomed to feel irritation or a desire for chat. So far from giving us a gloomy impression of the conditions of living, this is curiously exhilarating and enlarging. Sometimes we cannot avoid being ourselves, sometimes we can. Karenin has always led a mental life, outside the physical world, looking askance at the robust calves of the footmen, thinking "how strong and healthy they all are physically." When the catastrophe occurs and "real life," as he thinks of it, breaks in, he suddenly experiences the intense enjoyment of physical emotion and this gives him a sort of moral grandeur. He is a different man.

It is because of this absurd and marvellous complexity that we can accept so easily the intrusion of Tolstoy's own explanations. He is obviously telling us himself that what made Karenin's new moral fineness and calm impossible for long was the "coarse power" of social pressure. "The very thing that had been a source of suffering to him had become a spiritual joy . . . but as time went on he saw that however natural his position might

30 / John Bayley

appear to him at the time, he would not be allowed to remain in it." This suggests that Karenin has found, what Tolstoy himself always wanted to find, a clear and simple solution to his troubles, and that only society prevents it. Tolstoy calmly ignores the fact, so abundantly clear from the previous pages, that Karenin's own nature, necessarily complex as it is, would soon disrupt his present calm without any help from society.

The stasis in which he does eventually repose, with the help of quack religion and Lydia Ivanovna, is that of a very ordinary hypocrisy and self-righteousness. It seems to be something of a relief to Tolstoy to get him settled in this way, for he has shown every sign of being a fascinating and uncontrollable figure. Though his disposal is convincing, he is disposed of: he is removed from the area of the novel in which development takes place, and in which the involuntary revelations of Tolstoy's analytic art can still intrigue and disconcert us. He might be said to be carried forward into the pages of *Resurrection*, for he becomes the type of figure we meet with in that novel.

His disposal was important for the final version of Tolstoy's plot. His refusal to divorce Anna has no effect on the outcome. Anna has refused the offer of divorce when he was in his forgiving mood because she needed—if she were to escape—to think of him not as she did when she was ill but as she had done during the first period of her love for Vronsky. If he had forgiven her and wished her well, Anna could not have shaken him off as one might shake off a drowning man. "That other one was drowned; of course it was wrong, but it had been the only way of escape."

Tolstoy had originally planned that she should feel remorse for "that good man," her husband, and that this would help to destroy her subsequent marriage to Vronsky. She would have felt guilty towards both men, and tormented by the continued presence of both in her life. In this version Karenin must remain capable of the exalted mood in which he forgave Anna when her daughter was born. That mood must in fact be a reaction based not on the physical temperament, of which Tolstoy is a master, but on the oddities of the psyche, where he is far less at home. The triangle would persist with its three sides in a highly dramatic relation to each other, and Karenin in the role of Dostoevsky's "eternal husband." Karenin haunts the new ménage. In spite of the pain it gives him he goes out of his way to see the pair at social gatherings. Vronsky is not happy, and goes into society by himself. Distracted and jealous, Anna reflects that there is nothing for her but to enjoy the so-called pleasures of life, and thinks even of running away with Yashvin, whom she knows to be secretly in love with her. Karenin, having heard talk at a party of murders inspired by jealousy, buys a pistol. He goes to see Anna and urges her to return to him, not for his sake or hers, but because they have broken the sacrament of marriage. Christ has saved him, by enabling him to pardon her, and will save her too. He bursts into tears. At this moment Vronsky comes back from the ballet. Karenin rushes out. Anna says to Vronsky: "He has come as a spiritual director, believing me to be unhappy." "That's very decent of him," sneers Vronsky, and goes on to accuse Karenin of false emotionalism and hypocrisy. Anna defends him passionately, and there is a violent quarrel which leads to Anna's suicide.

The interest of these early scenarios is their resemblance to Tolstoy's plays, particularly to his last one, *The Live Corpse*. Significantly, both the *idea* of the novel's early drafts, and of the play, resulted in an externalisation of character—we can no more imagine Tolstoy entering into these persons than he could enter the persons initially conceived of in terms of appearance— the buxom sloe-eyed jolie laide, and her bald blue-chinned lover. Moreover, the scenario shows him taking the emotions seriously, as it were, and resolving the plot by means of them. The dramatist cannot afford to question the absoluteness of the emotions out of which his drama is concocted. Henry James's great "scenario" novels—*The Wings of the Dove* and *The Golden Bowl*— require a necessary faith in the permanence of states like love and forgiveness— these things cannot be allowed to disappear or modify under examination, because the drama depends on them for its poignancy and point. Similarly, in *The Live Corpse*, which uses a variant of the triangular situation of the early *Anna* scenario, Tolstoy accepts the scenario convention in order to secure a dramatic effect and also score a forensic point about marriage as a social institution. Karenin the virtuous lover of *The Live Corpse* (the coincidence of names reveals the relation to the *Anna* scenario) is simply "in love" with the married heroine. The nature and quality of this love cannot be analysed and hence this Karenin cannot acquire true Tolstoyan life as a character. The "live corpse" himself, the heroine's erratic husband, Fedya, wishes to disappear in order to leave her free to marry her virtuous lover, and in order that he himself may live with a gipsy girl. And again, this determination is not an aspect of his character but a necessity of the plot: he is assumed to give the "truth" about himself when he states that he hates his wife because he has done her harm, and loves the gipsy because he has given her money and done her good.

In the completed *Anna* there are no such truths, only people. Their full realisation by Tolstoy deprives of relevance all the novelist's willed conceptions and plottings, all the dramatist's confrontations and planned crises. For the last time in Tolstoy's art the work comes clean away from its shapings and intentions, as the statue from the marble. For the last time we feel a total difference in kind, and not merely in the degree of development, between the conception and the completed work. Its final self no longer seems to belong to Tolstoy, nor to be capable of being affected by him. The characters "do what is·in their nature to do": they are invulnerable to the author's powers of choice. Unthinkable for Anna to contemplate an affair with Yashvin, or for Karenin to visit her and urge her to return to him — unthinkable because such elements of the accidental and unpredictable would send them back to the tentative beginnings of Tolstoy's process, from which our knowledge of them, as people, has so completely emancipated them.

Chance and Design in *Anna Karenina*

Robert Louis Jackson

In chapter 18, part 1, of *Anna Karenina*, some seventy pages from the beginning of the novel, Tolstoy introduces Anna to the reader for the first time
in person. The scene is a Moscow railroad station. Stepan Oblonsky is there
to meet his sister Anna who is arriving from Petersburg; Vronsky, to meet
his mother who is arriving on the same train. All four meet, exchange
amenities, and prepare to leave the station; momentarily, a disturbing incident draws their attention: a railroad guard has been crushed by one of the
cars. After a brief delay (Vronsky leaves some money for the guard's family),
the group departs.

Chance seems to rule this occasion: Vronsky and Oblonsky, though ac-
quainted, have met by chance at the station. Anna, it turns out, had been
entrusted by her husband to Vronsky's mother at the Petersburg station and
they have made the trip together. Vronsky's meeting with Anna, then, is
fortuitous. The death of the guard, apparently, also is an accident.

A view of the surface, or visible structure, of this chapter reflects the
unplanned or "natural" character of the action: people alight from a train
and greet other people; bits of conversation seem to advance in a kind of
meandering movement—in short, build up a sense of the ritualistic, yet banal
and basically unstructured character of most meetings and departures at railroad
stations. The dramatic incident—the death of the guard, which takes up the
final portion of this slight chapter—explodes the sense of the casual and ordinary; it provides a momentary focus of attention for the characters. Yet
its sudden and alarming intrusion into the casual routine serves only to increase

From *The Disciplines of Criticism*, edited by Peter Demetz, Thomas Greene, and Lowry Nelson,
Jr. © 1968 by Yale University. Yale University Press, 1968.

our feeling of the unplanned in chapter 18. Our impression of the unplanned, however, is precisely an impression: on closer analysis it gives way to a sense of organized movement and design. The action, seen from the artist's point of view, is coherent and saturated with content.

The unifying element in the chapter, indeed its axis, must be sought in Anna. She is the primary focus of the artist's attention; her embryonic relationship with Vronsky constitutes the motive force for the inner action of the chapter. In this action Anna's character is free to attract, magnetize, and, in this sense, introduce "order" in the field of personalities around her; but in this action, also, character is revealed as a determined shape, as an embodiment of an already existing fate. We may define Tolstoy's purpose in chapter 18, then, as twofold: to disclose those elements of character in Anna which are her fate, and to capture that moment when, under the impact of character and the changes brought about through encounter, the elements of chance group themselves into coherent design. To present this whole action, without allowing its inner dynamics to obtrude upon, or overwhelm, the "natural" and free flow of surface action—here is the real art of Tolstoy.

At the opening of chapter 18, Vronsky steps up to the door of a train compartment and stops in order to make way for a lady who is coming out. He glances "at the exterior of this lady" who obviously belongs to the upper classes, begs her pardon, and is about to enter the carriage when he feels the need to have another look at her, "not because she was very beautiful, not because of the elegance and modest grace which were evident in her whole person, but because there was something particularly caressing and tender in the expression of her lovely face when she passed him."

Not so much exterior beauty or elegance as a certain compelling interior richness of being, a refined sensuousness defines Anna. Tolstoy's emphasis here is carried over into the crucial characterization of Anna as seen through Vronsky. Anna turns to look at Vronsky and her dark eyes rest momentarily upon him in a friendly, attentive manner. She then turns to the approaching crowd as if in search of someone.

> In that brief glance Vronsky had time to notice a restrained animation which played over her face. . . . It was as though her nature were so brimming over with an abundance of something that against her will it expressed itself now in a radiant look, now in a smile. She deliberately shrouded the light in her eyes, but it gleamed against her will in a barely perceptible smile.

Tolstoy has drawn Vronsky—and the reader—into the interior of Anna's being. He now calls attention to the welling up from it of a vital life force: animation (*ozhivlenie*) — a key word used three times in chapter 18 in descriptions of Anna. But it is "restrained animation"; it is held back by "will," and yet it makes itself felt "against her will." Precisely this force of energy, this vitality, this almost animal animation is a distinguishing mark of Anna. At the moment Vronsky meets Anna, these opposite forces of animation and restraint ("will") are in delicate equilibrium; at the end of the chapter, when Anna leaves the station, that equilibrium has been lost.

Contradiction, conflict, tension between opposite elements, then, is evident in Anna's nature from the outset; it also enters into her social perspective. Tolstoy brings this out obliquely in the scene under discussion. Vronsky, after exchanging glances with Anna, steps into the train, greets his mother, and, while talking with her, overhears a conversation of a woman (Anna) with a man outside the door.

> "All the same [*vsë-taki*], I do not agree with you," said the voice of the woman.
> "That's the Petersburg way of looking at it, Madame."
> "Not the Petersburg way, but simply a woman's way."
> "Well, anyway, permit me to kiss your hand."

These are the first words uttered by Anna in the novel. We do not know the subject of dispute, but this makes it possible for the words to produce a more general impression upon us. Almost the first word, vsë-taki, superbly establishes that singular quality of contrariety which will define, in a sense, Anna's whole stance before society; vsë-taki (all the same, nonetheless, however that may be) is a word which implies some kind of concession, perhaps, in the sphere of logic, but thereupon indicates clearly a stubborn adherence to one's own point of view in spite of logic or of convincing counterargument. The little colloquy we have quoted serves also to raise the problem content of Anna's nature to a general intellectual and social level — the level of action of the novel as a whole. What emerges from the colloquy is the image of a woman of tenacious viewpoint, one who rejects identification, significantly, with a "Petersburg" outlook, but who firmly embraces the "woman's" point of view. The polarity here of Petersburg and the "woman's" point of view anticipates the major confrontation of Anna in the novel.

Assertiveness, decisiveness, the readiness to take the lead — these are essential qualities of Anna, and they are manifested throughout her relationship with Vronsky. Tolstoy at the very first appearance of Anna in the novel signals these qualities. Vronsky introduces himself to Anna: "You probably don't remember me." "On the contrary," Anna replies.

"I should have recognized you—your mother and I, it seems, talked of nothing but you the whole journey," she said, at last allowing the animation that sought release to express itself in a smile. "But still no sign of my brother."

"Do go and call out for him, Alesha," said the old Countess.

Vronsky went out onto the platform and shouted: "Oblonsky! here!"

But Madame Karenina did not wait for her brother and, as soon as she caught sight of him she stepped down from the train with a resolute step. And, as soon as her brother reached her she flung her left arm around the neck of her brother, with a movement that struck Vronsky by its resoluteness and grace, and drawing him quickly to her warmly kissed him. Vronsky could not take his eyes off her and, without knowing why, smiled. But recollecting that his mother was waiting for him, he went back again into the train.

Animation, decisiveness, directness—these qualities of character in Anna are expressed in her physical actions and being as well. What is equally striking in this episode, however, is Tolstoy's emphasis upon Anna's independence. Her readiness to initiate action, significantly, contrasts with the merely responsive action of Vronsky. He steps out onto the platform in response to his mother's request; Anna, on the other hand, "did not wait for her brother." Further, it is in this passage that Tolstoy calls attention to a pattern in Vronsky's relationship with his mother. The final line in the passage cited—"But recollecting that his mother was waiting for him, he went back again into the train"—is the first embodiment, however slight, of a motif sounded at the conclusion of chapter 17, part 1: the purely external obeisance and respect Vronsky accords his mother.

This motif, which Tolstoy weaves into the very texture of the most casual actions of Vronsky, forms a brilliant yet eminently natural prelude to the exchange between Vronsky and his mother on "le parfait amour." Vronsky's mother lets fall a veiled hint apropos of the value of a liaison with a woman like Anna, coupling it with an indirect disapproval of his courting of Kitty. Though Vronsky is irritated by his mother's remarks he in fact does break off his courtship of Kitty and strikes up an affair (though not in the cynical spirit of his mother) with Anna. The motif of Vronsky's curious social attachment to his mother's person rises to the surface once again in the exchange which follows between Anna and Vronsky's mother on the question of getting along without their sons. Vronsky's mother tells Anna not to worry about her son: "You cannot expect never to be parted"—a remark, of course, that would be better directed to herself and her own obvious concern over Vronsky's apparent interest in Kitty.

The final episode of the chapter serves to bring into sharper relief the characters of Anna and Vronsky. Anna and her brother, as well as Vronsky and his mother, prepare to leave the station when they learn of the guard's accident. Vronsky and Oblonsky follow the crowd to find out about the accident. They return:

> Oblonsky and Vronsky had both seen the disfigured corpse. Oblonsky, plainly, was suffering. His face was distorted and he seemed ready to burst into tears.
>
> "Oh, what a horror! Oh, Anna, if you had seen it! Oh, what a horror!" he kept repeating.
>
> Vronsky was silent and his handsome face was serious, but perfectly tranquil.
>
> "Ah, if you had seen it, Countess," said Stepan Arkadich. "And his wife is here. It was awful to see her. She threw herself on the body. They say that he supported a huge family. There's the horror of it all!"
>
> "Can't something be done for her," Anna said in an agitated whisper.
>
> Vronsky looked at her and immediately left the train.
>
> "I'll be right back, Maman," he added, looking around in the doorway.

The passage lightly but deftly discloses something essential to the character of all participants. "Oblonsky, plainly, was suffering. His face was distorted and he seemed ready to burst into tears." There are no profundities to Oblonsky, yet his reaction is typical of his open, good-hearted, and somewhat two-dimensional nature. His emotions are near the surface and are easily—if not permanently—touched. Anna's "agitated whisper" and her immediate practical concern for the wife of the guard reveal both the depths of her responsiveness to human misfortune and the generosity of her nature. Both Oblonsky's and Anna's reactions have a direct verbal and even physical character. In striking contrast, Vronsky is silent and his handsome face, though serious, "perfectly tranquil."

Is there a dimension of human experience closed to Vronsky, this eminently decent and honorable gentleman? Unquestionably there is. What is involved here is a certain shallowness, broadly cultural, perhaps, and not one of basic intelligence; even more, a certain unconscious yet organic egoism which prevents him from communicating, or empathizing, with the full depth of feeling of another. The only moment when Vronsky's face will definitely lose its physical composure—a tranquillity which seems to define his limitations—is in his final appearance, after Anna's suicide, at a railroad station. Kozdnyshev scans the "obviously suffering face of Vronsky." Is Vronsky responding, here, to the tragedy of Anna? Has Anna's action finally broken through the composure of his face and being? It is difficult to answer this question with a yes or a no. It is of paramount significance, however, that Tolstoy observes of Vronsky on this occasion that "a gnawing toothache . . . impeded his speech." Tolstoy's own point of view is clear. He has lowered the plane of Vronsky's suffering—yet not arbitrarily, not maliciously, but fully in accord with the essential nature of Vronsky.

Anna questions whether something could not be done for the family of the guard. "Vronsky looked at her and immediately left the train." But the glance here is not one of common sentiment; it is only a glance of recognition of Anna's request. Vronsky does not share Anna's deep response to the disaster, and he will never understand or reach Anna at that deeper level on which her question was formulated. He will never really succeed in communicating with her. And this is one of the essential elements, of course, in the tragedy of Anna.

Vronsky, gentleman that he is, goes off to fulfill Anna's request, but man that he is, he characteristically leaves the money with an official without indicating that it should be used for the family of the deceased guard. As he leaves to fulfill his duty, he remarks: "I'll be right back, Maman." In a sense, Vronsky's whole relationship with Anna opens on a note of his mother's approval and ends with a return to mother. How important Tolstoy viewed the motif of Vronsky's concern for his mother may be judged alone by the reemergence of this motif in full force at the moment of Vronsky's final break with Anna:

> "It's a matter of complete indifference to me what your mother thinks and how she wants to marry you off," she said, putting down the cup with a trembling hand.
> "But we're not talking about that."
> "No, precisely about that. And let me assure you that I have no interest in a heartless woman—whether she be an old lady or not, your mother or somebody else—and I don't want to have anything to do with her."
> "Anna, I beg you not to speak disrespectfully of my mother."
> "A woman whose heart does not tell her wherein lies the hap-

piness and honor of her son—such a woman has no heart."

"I repeat my request that you do not speak disrespectfully about my mother, whom I respect," he said, raising his voice and looking at her severely. . . .

"You don't love your mother. Those are all words, words, words!" she said looking at him with hate.

(chap. 25. part 7)

The theme of respect for his mother, in short, the problem of comme il faut behavior and morality, points to a permanent concern of Tolstoy: the disjunction between form and content (and the atrophy of the latter) in the aristocratic, Petersburg world. Vronsky's unwillingness and inability to come to terms with this hyprocrisy in his relations with his mother points to the permanent ambiguity that marks his attitude toward Anna's rebellion, on the one hand, and society on the other. It is because Anna, both in her essential nature and her actions, refuses to tolerate this disjunction of form and content, this rule of hypocrisy and facade, because she insists on full integrity in choice and action, that she pays the price of "vengeance." "You're very much a whole man [tsel'nyj chelovek]," Oblonsky remarks on one occasion to Levin. "It's your virtue and your shortcoming." The same words, of course, may be applied to Anna.

At their last meeting, Vronsky fails to measure the depth of Anna's anxiety and despair and goes away thinking: " 'I've tried everything . . . only one thing remains, to pay no attention,' and he began to get ready to go to the city and then to his mother's again, to get her signature to the power of attorney." Do we not find here, perhaps, the solution to the enigma of Vronsky's composure at the scene of the accident? In the face of an event or situation that does not yield to rational endeavor, or of one that is beyond the reach of one's feelings, *to pay no attention*?

The conclusion of chapter 18, centering on Anna's reaction to the accident of the guard, provides a brilliant psychological climax to the chapter. Anna gets into the carriage, her lips trembling, barely restraining her tears. Her brother asks her what is the matter.

"It's a bad omen," she said.

"What nonsense!" said Stepan Arkadich. "You've come, that's the main thing. You can't imagine how I count on you."

"And have you known Vronsky for a long time?" she asked.

"Yes. You know we hope that he will marry Kitty."

"Really?" Anna said quietly. "Well, now let's talk about you,"

she added, shaking her head as though she wanted physically to
drive away something extraneous, oppressive.

How are we to interpret Anna's remark, "It's a bad omen"? Of central importance in any analysis of it is the fact that it is evoked in the context of
her meeting with Vronsky. A major preoccupation of Tolstoy throughout
chapter 18 is to record the mutual interest of Vronsky and Anna in its embryonic, at first almost unconscious phases. This interest, which first manifests
itself almost entirely in terms of basic physical instinct, then rises to the conscious game of "coquetry," suddenly is recognized for what it is by Anna
("she, obviously, did not want to continue in this tone") and suppressed,
driven underground, only to reappear again, almost involuntarily, in another
seemingly irrelevant context. Anna's remark, "Have you known Vronsky
long?" at the time of the accident suddenly makes us aware that the appearance
of Vronsky has destroyed the internal equilibrium that seems to have been
manifest in the tension of animation and restraint. The impact of the accident in the context of her encounter with Vronsky has aroused in her a disturbing and pessimistic awareness of her own situation. The thoughts that
Anna wishes almost physically to drive away are, of course, not at all "extraneous" to her nature, but of its very essence. Oblonsky's twice-repeated
remark at this juncture that he is counting on Anna (*nadejus' na tebja, vsja
nadezhda na tebja*) to resolve his marital difficulties, have — in retrospect — a
tragic irony to them.

It is obvious that Anna's remark, "it's a bad omen," is drawn from the
permanent depths of her nature. It reflects a feature of her personality which
the reader often notes: what Dolly calls Anna's "too gloomy" way of looking at things, or what Princess Betsy suggests is Anna's "tendency to look
at things too much in a tragic light." There is even a kind of Greek fatality
to the character and outlook of Anna. Restlessly, actively, almost physically,
she seeks out and creates her own reality, or realm, to play out her drama.
The play of chance — such play as we noted at the outset of our essay — is
more of an illusion than reality. For such a type as Anna, moreover, the
opportunity of chance only provides a consciously or unconsciously anticipated
opening; for such a person (Lermontov explored a very extreme example of
this type in Pechorin) chance is *fate*. Anna's comment, "it's a bad omen,"
is of course a perfect illustration of this active, willed transformation into
fateful actuality of one of those infinite and endlessly drifting bits of chance
that reality has in continual reserve.

Oblonsky, for his part, responds to Anna's comment on the level of
his own ache — the domestic drama which brings Anna to Moscow. He finds

it ridiculous to see in the accident of the guard a "bad omen" for the resolution of his problems. His response, "what nonsense!" reflects more than just the sober approach of the reasonable man to an admittedly quite subjective and, outwardly at least, superstitious reaction; it serves also to distinguish for us, albeit in a rudimentary and preliminary way, the ordinary consciousness from the one with tragic potential. Tolstoy's instructive juxtaposition of Anna and Oblonsky in this interchange, of course, is part of his whole contrast between Anna's tragic drama and Oblonsky's bourgeois domestic drama, or melodrama.

Chapter 18, then, may be regarded as constituting in microcosm the action of the novel as a whole as it pertains to Anna. The movement of the chapter from the buoyant, physically animated, and emotionally surcharged Anna, who steps down from the train, to the emotionally distraught, inward Anna of the chapter's conclusion paraphrases the fall of Anna in the novel at large; it lays the psychological and social groundwork for her real suicide toward the end of the novel. At the end of chapter 18 the purity of Anna's animation has been compromised and the tragic interiority of her nature revealed; by the end of the novel Anna's "tendency to look at things too much in a tragic light" has become a pathological phenomenon enveloping her entire world view in darkness.

The principle of realism guiding Tolstoy in this chapter, as elsewhere in his work, is one which Chekhov will develop to the highest point of perfection: the view that our casual everyday appearance, behavior, conversation—in short, our everyday "character" and confrontations—contain, reflect, anticipate the larger shape of our destiny. An old notion, of course (and one expressed by Heraclitus: "A man's character is his fate"), but one rarely embodied in art with consummate artistic mastery. Much of what will be recognized as the typical behavior and action of both Anna and Vronsky is discernible in embryonic form in this opening phase of their relationship.

The beauty of the chapter lies in Tolstoy's ability to maintain a primary focus upon the "natural" movement of surface action, of ordinary and casual encounter and conversation, while at the same time revealing in this seemingly routine material the texture of a dynamic reality rapidly acquiring design and shape. The themes of Anna and also, to some extent, those of Vronsky culminate in the episode of the accident. Here we have an explosion which momentarily smashes the "natural" calm of everyday life and behavior and brings to the surface the full, usually hidden, content of reality: in a single stroke Tolstoy reveals the tragic outlines of the future. The significance of the chapter as it pertains to Anna is summed up in its final episode: the death of the guard signals the birth of the tragic Anna.

The problem of the accident of the guard, indeed, Tolstoy's whole choice of the railroad station as a stage to introduce Anna, deserves some discussion. The fact that the image of the guard recurs to Anna and that she ultimately commits suicide in the same fashion as the guard only points to Tolstoy's vital preoccupation with the psychological motivation of Anna's suicide. But why, specifically, the death of a railroad guard, why a railroad station? Here Tolstoy's concern is not only with the dramatic and psychological potential of his material (this potential, after all, could be found elsewhere) but also with its *social* content and implications. The accident of the guard is a symbol and an embodiment—in Tolstoy's novelistic world view—not of some irrational, metaphysical factor in existence that may at any moment strike us down, but of the rational disorder of modern social and economic existence. It is of cardinal significance that two or three of the most traumatic moments of Anna's existence are played out in interaction with the harsh and discordant rhythms of the railroad. The iron railroad, or jarring train, as a symbol of dislocation of life, as an embodiment of new forces ruthlessly destroying the old patterns of patriarchal existence, becomes in *Anna Karenina* (as it does later, in a more didactic way, in *The Kreutzer Sonata*) a kind of symbol for the disorders of individual and family existence.

The accident of the guard is for Tolstoy not an occurrence of chance (except in the sense that it happens today and not tomorrow, to this guard and not to that one); it emerges, as a concrete possibility, from the actuality of a modern capitalist existence, that "external civilization" which increasingly alienates man from the products of his labor, from the sense of "usefulness" of his labor, and from those organic harmonies of man and labor which Tolstoy extols in his famous collective mowing scene in *Anna Karenina*. (When Levin asks that "we try to think of labor not in the European way," not as "abstract man *power*, but as the *Russian peasant* with his instincts," he is appealing also for a rational humanization of the labor process, a return to the "useful" labor of a patriarchal, agricultural existence.) Anna's suicide, likewise, is the final result of an alienation which for Tolstoy is rooted socially in the same dislocations and contradictions that the railroads bring to Russian life, dislocations which somehow acquire a unique and terrifying embodiment (in all its abstraction and senselessness and brutality) in the accident or suicide of the guard.

The shrieking chaos, the blinding play of lights and shadows, the choking sensations, the madly fluctuating temperatures and weird visual imagery of the night train back to St. Petersburg—to take another illustration of the same problem in *Anna Karenina*—not only accompanies but defines, one might almost say induces, Anna's annihilating moral crisis at that moment. "Then something screeched and clattered in a fearful way, as though somebody were being torn to pieces." The rending of her moral consciousness—for on this train trip, in fact, she breaks through the moral barrier—is significantly accompanied by a sense of upheaval and distortion throughout her being and by a terrifying sense of self-alienation: "And what am I doing here? Am I myself or somebody else?" We have an anticipation here of that total psychological and social alienation that Anna experiences in the period just before her suicide.

Of course, as we have noted, Anna's tragedy is firmly rooted in her own peculiar nature: her decision to commit suicide, as well as her choice of a particular form of suicide, may and must be explained in terms of her nature and of her unique personal history in which chance plays a role (though a minimal one). In short, there had to be a particular person of the nature of Anna Karenina and a particular combination of personal circumstances for there to have been a tragedy of the kind we have in this novel. But it is no less true that the Anna we know is inseparable from the problem content of the Russian society in which she lives; her rebellion, indeed the specific character of that rebellion, is in large part determined by the society which is the object of her rebellion.

In the light of these considerations, chapter 18 emerges as one of the most important and decisive ones in the novel. Here we have both "complication" and denouement. For the death of the guard and the death of Anna in the stupendous social perspective of Tolstoy are neither mutually detached phenomena nor accidents of chance, but—the one inert, the other conscious— inelectable phenomena of a society, like the obsessed Ahab, rushing toward catastrophe on iron rails.

In the final summation, one recognizes a distinct parallel and ultimate convergence in the lines of personal, that is, psychological, and also social motivation or fatality in Anna Karenina. It is precisely the convergence and organic unity of these lines that provides the tragedy of Anna with its depth, its amplitude, in the final analysis, its grandeur. Yet in positing the overwhelming elements of psychological and social fatality we do not deny the indispensable elements of freedom in Anna's tragedy. This freedom lies in the conscious choice of a tragic destiny. This will to meet one's destiny (which for the novelist Tolstoy is always concrete, social, historical) is a will to reach out and exemplify one's personal fate through an exploration of the limits of one's reality. A character exercises his enormous potential of freedom— and there are moments of critical choice—when he chooses to explore these limits, whether out of a sense of a lofty ideal, a sense of personal injustice, or a feeling of incompleteness. Such a character, on the subjective plane, tests his freedom and discovers his inherent fatality. But objectively such a character rises above the purely individual and pedestrian precisely because his discovered fate embodies more of the *necessity* of social existence. Anna, of course, is revealed in this unique, tragic perspective, one which, through its total illumination of reality, seems to transcend fatality itself.

Not without reason did Dostoevsky refer to Tolstoy as a "god of art."

Tolstoy's Underground Woman:
A Study of *Anna Karenina*

Willis Konick

In Moscow, Karenin, who has gone to seek a divorce, pursue bureaucratic intrigue, and escape his intolerable family situation, receives a telegram from Anna. She claims to be dying, and asks that he return and forgive her. Harsh and pitiless, Karenin reckons that to pardon would be sham, but to ignore her plea, and face the remote likelihood of her death, might disturb his future calm. He resolves to return to Petersburg, frankly wishing for her death, appalled to learn she has successfully given birth to a daughter, and lives on in fever and crisis. But when he is brought to her, a sudden witness to her tears, her need to punish that "other woman" who tempted her to indifference, cruelty, his mood changes; in the presence of the weeping and penitent Vronsky, Karenin gives way to his inherent faculty for deep, unequivocal response, reclines his head in the bend of Anna's arm, and forgives unceasingly, unrestrictedly, not only forgives Anna's sin but, at Anna's request, draws Vronsky to him, grasps the hand of the adulterer, and forgives him as well. It is a scene of great emotional power, one of the most striking in *Anna Karenina* and one which long remains in the reader's memory. I particularly remember this scene as I saw it many years back during a theatrical presentation of the novel at the Moscow Art Theatre. The production, which limited itself to Anna's story alone, was unfortunately false in most respects, false to the spirit of the novel, full of actors striking empty poses and reciting empty speeches. But as I watched and fidgeted I kept hoping that the scene of childbirth, the scene of Anna's near death would work; it was so naturally dramatic, so full of emotional meaning, that even the bad acting and prevailing

---

From *Russian and Slavic Literature,* edited by Richard Freeborn. © 1976 by Slavica Publishers, Inc.

disposition to melodrama could not entirely rob it of life. And true enough, when it came, the actors, as if sensing a dramatic peak had arrived, attempted some degree of restraint. There was Anna, writhing on her bed, speaking that great speech on forgiveness, and Karenin seated next to her, his head bent, and Vronsky behind them, covering his face with his hands. Everything proceeded exactly as it had in the novel, yet strangely enough I found it not moving but repulsive, embarrassing, worse than all the distortions that had preceded it. I left the theatre in a sour mood, and attributed my disappointment to the difficulties involved in adapting so complex a work for the stage.

Years later, while teaching the novel, I reread the scene and fall into that same sour temper I recall so vividly from my evening in the theatre. Might Tolstoy, in some measure, have intended to arouse precisely this mood? Does this magnificent and climactic scene of forgiveness and self-discovery, this artistically subtle reversal of roles, as a commanding and sympathetic Karenin faces a subdued Vronsky, turn into a parody of absolution? But Karenin's pardon is certainly genuine: Tolstoy has long prepared us for his susceptibility to tears; we already know that he teeters on the brink of an abyss, and now he has simply fallen in, to discover greater spiritual resources than we might have guessed. And Vronsky's defeat is entirely plausible; he himself recognizes that Karenin's adoption of Christian forgiveness transforms the dull cuckold and disarms the sophisticate. Might the source of our annoyance, our vague misgivings, be Anna herself? It is she who, however innocently, inspires tenderness in one man and mortification in the other. When Karenin first enters it is she who gazes upon him with new affection and declares: "I am still the same. But there is another woman in me, I'm afraid of her: it was she who fell in love with that man, and I tried to hate you, and I could not forget the self that had once been. I'm not that woman. Now I'm my real self, all myself. I'm dying now, I know I am; you ask him. I feel it already. . . . I only want one thing—for you to forgive me, forgive me completely!" Despite her fears, Karenin instantly relents; she puts her arms around him, raises her eyes "defiantly" and states: "there, I knew he would be like that! Now good-bye everyone, goodbye!" The doctor calms her, she rests more quietly and speaks again:

> "Remember one thing: that I only wanted your forgiveness, nothing more. . . . Why doesn't he come?" she cried, turning to Vronsky at the door. "Come in, come in! Give him your hand."
> Vronsky approached the side of the bed and seeing Anna, buried his face in his hands again.
> "Uncover your face! Look at him! He is a saint," she said. "Yes,

yes, uncover your face!" she cried angrily. "Alexei Alexandrovich, uncover his face! I want to see him."

Karenin took Vronsky's hands and drew them away from his face, terrible with its look of agony and shame.

"Give him your hand. Forgive him."

Karenin held out his hand, not attempting to restrain the tears that streamed down his cheeks.

"Thank God, thank God!" she cried, "now everything is ready. I will just stretch my legs a little. There, that's nice . . . Oh, God, oh God, when will it end? Give me some morphia! Doctor, give me morphia! Oh God, oh God!"

And she began tossing about in the bed.

All kinds of unpleasant thoughts occur as one reads these lines. One can well understand Anna's suffering and fear—she is terribly ill, after all—but she does rather expertly prepare for her own death, laying down conditions, extracting promises, setting her affairs in proper order ("now everything is ready"). There is something of the stage-manager about her, as she compels the two men to perform her bidding. And while the moralist might applaud Anna's decision to condemn that "other woman," to defy the adulteress, one might also expect more sympathy for Vronsky. Most curiously, she tells Karenin she wishes only one thing, his forgiveness, and then, grown calm, she discovers that she wants yet another thing, that Karenin forgive Vronsky as well, that Vronsky be brought from his hiding place and exposed to shame he can only erase by suicide. In this sense the scene prefigures her own actual death, and Vronsky's living suicide that follows.

Is such cruelly manipulative behavior born of Anna's present terror and anxiety, or is it fashioned from some earlier paradigm, which then remains reasonably constant throughout the novel? Is Anna the drowning man who grasps that death is only moments away and wildly flounders for support, or is she that figure on the ledge, poised high above the street, tensely observing the gathering audience below and the dismayed faces thrust from windows above, silently attending to the counsel of pastor and police, waiting until the anxiety of the crowd equals his own dread? The answer to this question will surely provide some definition of Anna's character. And since such definitions are already numerous—and contradictory—it might be well to pause at this point and summarize them.

As in all situations which aggravate man's natural opposition to his neighbor, there are hawks and doves on the question of Anna. The hard line is best expressed by M. S. Gromeka, whose long essay (or series of essays) on the novel appeared less than a decade after its publication. Gromeka finds much to pity in Anna and Vronsky and more to censure: in trying to legitimize their adulterous union they break the ineffable law of man's nature, and prepare their own destruction. As for Anna, she is simply a woman of fierce and criminal passion, who sacrifices her family, her social position and finally her own life in the name of love. Gromeka's outlook has remained a minority position, and the vast majority of commentators upon the novel prefer to view Anna as victim rather than felon. B. Eikhenbaum, in his study of Tolstoy in the seventies, compares Anna to the heroine of Ostrovsky's *The Storm*, and claims that "The further the novel approaches its conclusion, the more enigmatic Anna's guilt becomes. Anna is transformed from criminal to victim, and the natural question arises: why the epigraph 'Vengeance is mine, and I shall repay.'" V. Shklovskii enthusiastically states that "Anna Karenina stands in the novel separately from all others, above all others, because she loves as one really loves." John Bayley (in *Tolstoy and the Novel*) considers Anna neither "selfish" nor "vindictive" by nature, and suggests that she and Vronsky might still have made a go of it, had it not been for her terrible "sense of isolation." In his recent critical introduction to Tolstoy's works R. F. Christian speaks of the "warmth and sincerity" of Anna's character, of Tolstoy's own battle against "his rational urge to condemn her for breaking the rules." Undoubtedly there are moments in the novel which would seem to support the widespread suspicion that Tolstoy, despite his harsh epigraph, succumbed to the charm and vivacity of his heroine. Even the childbirth scene could accommodate this vision of Anna, had Tolstoy excluded Anna's peremptory stage directions. We might then rest quietly with Garbo's Anna, with Vivien Leigh's Anna, with the Moscow Art Theatre's Anna, with an Anna ravished by Vronsky, wasted by her husband, undone by her society, ruined by all those unable to respond to her full and passionate love. This Anna is ultimately compelled, out of her own desperation, to do their work and destroy herself: again, the drowning man rather than that figure poised, waiting, high on the ledge.

The contradictions intrinsic to such an interpretation of Anna are many. Could an author as careful, as deliberate as Tolstoy, grow so fuzzy about a heroine whose proper likeness occupied him through many drafts of the novel? And what of those grave inconsistencies in Anna's own behavior? She herself is aware of some of them, though blind to others, and when they grow too clamorous, too burdensome, she screws up her eyes and pushes them away from herself. Why does she so wildly veer from pole to pole like some crazed magnet? Is this merely characteristic of Anna late in the novel, when she truly does begin to see double, when her sense of her own identity grows so tenuous that the image she sights in the mirror no longer bears intimate connection to her own consciousness, when, trancelike, she raises her own hand to her lips and kisses it, as she might touch, caress the hand of another? Or does such curious behavior make its appearance much earlier in the novel? Certainly Anna arouses countless questions from the beginning, and at least three aspects of her nature become explicit shortly after we first meet her in Moscow. There is the alluring, vivacious figure who steps off the train and promptly enchants Vronsky, with all that "suppressed animation" darting "between her sparkling eyes and the slight smile curving her red lips." There is Anna the peacemaker who, through honest affection for both parties, brings the warring Dolly and Stiva together again. And there is Anna at the ball, more charming than ever, whom Kitty views from that vast distance born of competition and despair: "Yes, there is something strange, diabolical, and enchanting about her." Which of these three provides the source of future pain and doubt and passion, or do all three play a role? And why does Anna, out of all the young men she has met and will meet, select an officer so blank and typical, so handsomely cardboard as Vronsky? She herself, upon her return to Petersburg, cannot imagine anything between them, until that unaccountable excitement and vitality returns, to stretch her nerves "like strings around pegs," to cause her to see real objects as hazy, dislocated, transformed, a phenomenon she finds not terrifying but "rather pleasant." Later, lying in the darkness and thinking of Vronsky, she will seem to see the very brightness of her own eyes. Is there something dangerous as well as attractive in her newfound vivacity? We understand why she is displeased by her first sight of Karenin, after her return to Petersburg, with his ungainly walk, his protruding ears, his swollen veins, his habit of cracking his knuckles. But why does she find her son, whom she loves so unreservedly, also disappointing? "Just as her husband had done, her son produced on Anna a feeling akin to disappointment. In imagination she had pictured him nicer than he actually was. She had to descend to reality in order to enjoy him as he was." And why, later in the novel, when her passion for Vronsky rules her thoughts, must she invest him with greater appeal than he seems to possess? "She laid her hands on his shoulders, and gave him a long, searching look, her eyes full of love. She was studying his face, making up for the time she had not seen him, comparing, as she did every time they met, the picture of him in her imagination (incomparably superior, impossible in reality) with him as he actually was." Once she takes Vronsky as her lover, does she wholly despise her husband? Is she entirely accurate when she characterizes their previous years together as sham? We know she must now record each defect in him "because of the great wrong she was doing him." But we also know some kind of understanding must have once existed between them, perhaps a rather enviable one, for Karenin immediately perceives her new "impenetrable armor of falsehood," and recalls, not years of barren indifference, but a reservoir of mutual trust: "But for him, knowing her, knowing that when he was five minutes late in going to bed she would remark on it and ask the reason—who knew that she always immediately told him all her joys, pleasures, and sorrows—for him her reluctance now to notice his state of mind or say a word about herself signified a great deal. He saw that the depths of her soul, always before open to him, were now closed against him." Moreover Anna's recurrent dream, after what I shall call the "seduction scene," when she and Vronsky destroy the "first stage" of their love and commence their affair, is one in which both husband and lover play a significant part. "She dreamed that she was the wife of both of them and that both lavished their caresses on her. Alexei Alexandrovich was weeping, kissing her hands, and saying, 'How happy we are now!' and Alexei Vronsky was there too, and he, too, was her husband. And she was marvelling that this had once seemed impossible to her, and she would explain to them, laughing, that it was ever so much simpler this way and that now both of them were contented and happy. But this dream weighed on her like a nightmare and she awoke from it in terror." This wish-fulfilling dream, by the way, which assumes the proportions of nightmare in moments of wakefulness, will be realized in that very childbirth scene I spoke of earlier, as husband and lover gather at her bed, and Anna orders the conduct of the two Alexeis.

More questions arise. Why, after the seduction scene I refer to above, does Anna rather ominously warn Vronsky: "Everything is over . . . I have nothing but you left. Remember that." At this point any number of options still exist: she has not told her husband of her affair, and she certainly does not intend to relinquish her son. Or does she already begin to squeeze life of its alternatives, until she will be left only with raw, naked choice? And why later, at the scene of childbirth, does she also command Karenin to remember she wanted only his forgiveness, nothing more? Why does she swear at several points in the novel that she will never abandon her son and then, at the end of part 4, leave in headlong flight, with hardly a thought to the boy? Why, during the childbirth scene, does she condemn that "other woman," who led her to love Vronsky and then despise Karenin for his charity, find him a "loathsome presence"? How might one explain her curious behavior toward Vronsky after her visit to her son, in part 5 of the novel? First she seems to forget him entirely, then she experiences a new wave of love for him, and then, just as abruptly, she resolves to punish and hate him, to go to the opera and expose herself to public humiliation. Why do we find this mature, experienced and sophisticated woman, reunited with her son, "crying in the same thin childlike way as he"? And why, earlier in the novel, when she receives her husband's letter, sternly prohibitive but promising truce, when she feels she will not know "freedom in love," does she weep "unrestrainedly, as children weep when they are punished"? Why, after the depth of understanding she reveals to Dolly in Moscow, her acceptance of error, of occasional deflection from one's best and natural path, does she continually find herself in the unenviable position of loving two beings at once? If we are to believe the testimony of her dream, her yearning for husband and lover, she remains firmly wed to Karenin even after she and Vronsky commence their affair. And when the break with her husband arrives, she finds herself torn between equal passion for Vronsky and for her son. As she confesses to Dolly: "I love these two beings only, and the one excludes the other. I cannot have them both; yet that is my one need. And since I can't have that I don't care about the rest. Nothing matters, nothing, nothing!" Is it mere circumstance which visits such despair upon this woman, or does some pattern emerge, some terrifying need to embrace hopeless opposition? And, finally, why do we know so little of her former life, compared to all the other characters, who seem admirably ready to absorb their past and probe their future? Of her years with Karenin there are only hints, and of her life before that, her adolescence, even less. Only late in the novel, in a rare reflective moment, does Anna glimpse herself as a girl of seventeen, and ask "Was that really me, the girl with the red hands?" Such curious omissions led one critic to comment shrewdly: "To the very end Anna is a wonderful woman whose early history has never been fully explained" (Perry Lubbock, *The Craft of Fiction*).

Is there some context which might bear the weight of these incongruities, might explain such strangely inconstant behavior? There seems to lurk here some imperative need to make immoderate and imprudent requests of self and others, but it appears locked to equal fear of such demands. One hesitates to define this as the response of an unhappily neurotic woman; such labels customarily precede the dismissal of the character from the work of art, from one's field of vision. Yet in the terms of the writings of at least one psychoanalyst, a number of statements on the neurotic personality so conform to elements in Anna's character, that I must at least tentatively offer them here, in partial support of my hypothesis. The writer is Karen Horney, the book is *The Neurotic Personality of Our Time*, a thorough but not complex application of post-Freudian psychoanalytic theory, easily accessible to the layman and written with a minimum of jargon. In brief and compelling terms, Horney describes the neurotic condition as an "insidiously increasing, all-pervading feeling of being lonely and helpless in a hostile world," as a thirst for two contrary rewards: affection, and power and control. She understands that this need for affection can be easily misconstrued, and that all of us who have hoped for a little more love and warmth in life need not post ourselves at the analyst's door. "The difference," she cautions, "between love and the neurotic need for affection lies in the fact that in love the feeling of affection is primary, whereas in the case of the neurotic the primary feeling is the need for reassurance, and the illusion of loving is only secondary." Since Anna speaks of love constantly, until Vronsky, late in the novel, begs her to find a synonym, we might be on interesting ground here. Even more pertinent to Anna's nature is Horney's explanation of what she calls the need for unconditional love: "The neurotic wish for unconditional love . . . is much more comprehensive than the normal one, and in its extreme form it is impossible of fulfillment. It is a demand for love, literally without any condition or any reserve . . . a wish to be loved regardless of any provocative behavior." I hope to use these quotes from Horney to create some key, some structure which may guide us through those inconsistencies I spoke of earlier. But if the psychoanalytic mood seems gloomy or pretentious, one may merely think of Anna as a person who comes to deal in absolutes: unconditional demands, total fears, extremities of power and subservience, an unusual figure for Tolstoy at this stage of his career. Indeed, she might well be called Tolstoy's underground woman, not because Tolstoy shares theme or style with Dostoyevski, but because Anna, like the underground man, is the prime subversive force in the novel, inciting and alarming all others.

Quite early in the novel, much earlier than we might expect, we are offered Anna's own vision of a "cold and hostile" world. It is the morning after the races, the morning after she has told Karenin of her adulterous union with Vronsky, and has experienced the brief elation of telling the truth. Disconsolately she walks about the terrace of her summer home and ponders her future:

> "Can it be that they won't forgive me, won't understand how none of it could be helped?" she said to herself.
>
> Standing still and looking at the tops of the aspen-trees waving in the wind, with their rain-washed leaves glistening brightly in the cold sunshine, she knew that they would not forgive her, that everything and everybody would be merciless to her now as was this sky, these green trees. And again she felt that duality in her soul.

In marked contrast to such despair, to the imminent birth of a duality which forges each emotion, each human trait to its opposite, joy to hopelessness, self-confidence to perplexity, we have the Anna, much earlier on, who convinces Dolly to follow her first and best impulse, to return to her husband. Dolly has posed the fateful question, whether Anna might be equally forgiving of a husband's indiscretion. Anna replies:

> "I do not know, I cannot tell. . . . Yes, I can," said Anna, after a moment's consideration; and, capturing in her thought the situation and weighing it on her own inner scale (*uloviv mysl'iu polozhenie i svesiv ego na vnutrennikh vesakh*), she added: "Yes, I can, I can, I can. Yes, I should forgive. I would not be the same, no; but I should forgive, and forgive as utterly as if it had never happened, had never happened at all."

Could anything be more different than these two visions of Anna? Anna with Dolly is unquestionably Anna at her best, Anna as we shall seldom see her again, giving of herself, responding to others honestly and openly, but with a dutiful and necessary caution (not detachment). She still retains that happy facility for drawing back not in hesitation but in thought, so that she might gauge the demands of experience against her own inherent strength. For Anna staring at the aspen trees the inner scale has vanished; there are no decisions to be made, nothing against which to reckon one's strength; one can only acknowledge weakness and await defeat. How then was that inner scale abandoned—how and why? How could such a poised, confident woman lose the power to decide, the right to hope?

Certainly a partial answer to this question must lie in her "illicit" love, the union with Vronsky which forms shortly after her meeting with Dolly, and in her subsequent guilt and doubt, her quarrels with her husband, her concern for her son. With Seriozha as admonitory compass, Anna and Vronsky sail off into deep and troubled waters, Vronsky an experienced but not always attentive navigator, Anna an overwrought and queasy passenger. But must adulterous love bear such grievous consequences? Unlike Gromeka, Tolstoy does not yet seem in a mood to condemn; he keeps his distance and his equanimity, and permits Anna to make her choice. Obviously the earnest and moral Anna cannot enter into an affair with the easy abandon and good humor of Princess Betsy, but she can, with her good sense, her "inner scale" weigh her awakened passion for Vronsky, her loyalty to her husband, her deep affection for her son, and find each possesses considerable density, and manifest, though not equal, value. It will not make the conflict of loyalties any easier, and it will not erase her sense of guilt, but it will help her to make some necessary distinctions. At Princess Betsy's party, after her return to Petersburg, she seems almost ready to do so. The discussion is of love, various opinions are expressed, and Vronsky, now in pursuit, waits breathlessly for Anna's own response. Pausing for a moment she answers: "I think . . . that if there are as many minds as there are heads, then there are as many kinds of love as there are hearts." A sensible, intelligent position, and one Anna never returns to again; the more fully she enters into liaison with Vronsky, the more eagerly she embraces a new, dangerous and far more radical definition of love.

We catch a glimpse of this spectacular metamorphosis at the ball in Moscow, and it is Kitty who first senses the change in Anna. This assured and gracious woman grows suddenly intoxicated, as Kitty once was, with the spirit of the ball and the stimulation of conquest. It is not Anna alone whom Kitty observes, however, and her shock is far greater when she witnesses the transformation in Vronsky:

> Every time he spoke to Anna, her eyes lit up joyously and a smile of happiness parted her red lips. She seemed to be making an effort to restrain these signs of joy but in spite of herself they appeared on her face. "But what of him?" Kitty looked at him and was filled with dread. What was so plainly mirrored in Anna's face, she saw in him. What had become of his usually quiet, firm manner and tranquil, carefree expression? Now, every time he turned towards Anna, he bowed his head a little, as if he wanted to fall at her feet in adoration, and his eyes held only submission and fear. "I would not offend you," his every look seemed to say. "I only want to save myself but I do not know how." The expression on his face was one Kitty had never seen before.

The key to why Anna falls so abruptly in love with Vronsky, and precisely Vronsky, lies in that "look of adoration." She will recall it as she leaves for Petersburg on the train, and all the remembered excitement of the ball will return; she will contemplate it regularly as he pursues her about St. Petersburg. Nor will that adoration ever waver much, not until late in the novel when Vronsky, grown impatient with idolatry and surfeit with her beauty, will fret and sulk like any ordinary husband. Though he is very much the aggressor at the early stages of their affair, and generously possesses all those attractively masculine traits Karenin sorely lacks, he is, in his manly way, genuinely submissive when it counts, and yields to Anna's emotions on the occasion of every serious crisis — and there are many of them. He is unaccountably ready to share her tears. He immediately responds to her injunction that he come to her home, though he knows her husband has forbidden his presence there, that their accidental meeting will precipitate a new crisis (as it does). Again and again her feelings are promptly communicated to him; he acts as litmus paper for every threat to her own well-being: "In her presence he had no will of his own: without knowing the grounds for her distress, he already felt himself involuntarily infected by it." Such ready sympathy is powerfully appealing, of course, but for Anna it is bad medicine; Vronsky's adoration, right there at the ball, sparks that need in Anna for unconditional love, and once it has been awakened she can never go fully back to the woman she was before. Something stirs within her that has clearly lain dormant, unrecognized for years, perhaps all her life; once provoked it will increasingly demand its own special nourishment, it will seek to order its own affairs. Vronsky's worshipful gaze and her own vitality will lead her to that point where she loses mastery of herself, where her intelligence no longer works, where she can only gaze at the aspen trees and reflect on human malice.

I do not think such a sudden metamorphosis implausible, though its consequences for Anna are extreme. Who has not felt at least mild exhilaration when invested with new power: a love declared, a reward granted? At such moments our inner scales plunge precipitately to one side, and we experience an agreeable imbalance, just compensation for the neglect or indifference of others. Anna's response, however, is of a slightly different order; she is not only stimulated by the ball, by the attractive man with whom she dances and by the promise of submissiveness he offers, but she is also stirred by that twin imperative of which Horney speaks: the craving for affection and the craving for power and control. Newly alive, reborn in the very sparkle of her eyes, the only love now worthy of the name must rise from some source beyond her, and flow unceasingly and exclusively in her direction. Like the child who observes that, by tears, by naughtiness, by some childishly shrewd threat, some half-contrived, half-real accident, he may bring his parents to him, he may arouse their maximum love or attention, so Anna increasingly relies on tears and threats and scenes half-staged, half-real to draw forth the fullest response from Vronsky and, on occasion, from her husband. She herself will respond with all the sparkle and vivacity of the child, those short bursts of warmth and affection that make the child lovable. But, like the child, she also fears the very weapons she uses: tears may become the prelude to real suffering and remorse, and the accident, begun in artifice, may end in real hurt. And there is another fear more profound: that the parent will not respond, that the demand may prove too great, and the bedroom door will remain closed, the child will be left to weep alone with his cut, celebrating his loneliness in a thin, childish wail, like the cry Anna joins to her son's. Anna, returning home from Princess Betsy's gathering with Vronsky, after her impressive conclusion that there are as many loves as hearts, warns Vronsky that he had best not speak so easily of love, that the word means too much to her, and we surmise that those words spoken at Princess Betsy's spring from a different Anna, and that love, in her new sense, will require the totality of a Vronsky, or a Karenin, or a Seriozha. And as she consumes more she gives correspondingly less; her greed grows too great and her essential generosity of spirit, glimpsed in that scene with Dolly at the beginning of the novel, and her reason, which she can never entirely abandon, tell her she asks much and grants nothing in return. Her passion, her need to be placated, her ventures, often brilliantly successful, into managing the deeds of others are accompanied by spurts of self-hatred — "I am a bad woman, a wicked woman." She feels increasingly inadequate to the awesome task she has set for herself; to conceal, beneath affection's countenance, a quest for consummate power. But attempts to think through her dilemma grow too painful, and she must increasingly fling herself into new action. Even when she imagines herself most wholly the slave to others, there lies, quiescent, an unborn threat. Thus her "Remember that" to Vronsky, during the seduction scene, is not so much cautionary, a reminder of his new responsibilities, as a half-challenge, later to emerge in repeated challenges that he prove his love. Thus, in the childbirth scene, she asks her husband for just one thing — that he forgive her — and then, when that request has been granted, she is inspired to another, like the child who, having exacted one promise, tries the game anew. But once she gains Karenin's forgiveness — and no gift could be more totally unconditional — she loathes him for that very love, she is physically repulsed by his presence, she must escape at any cost, escape from her demand and his compliance. And there is yet another demand she must fulfill, a burden equally heavy: that she create beauty wherever she goes, her own beauty particularly, and that all ugliness, all disfigurement must be shut out. In Europe, where conditions are ideal, she turns her full attention upon Vronsky, creates an island of beauty, submerges, with unexpected ease, all consciousness of husband and son. After her return to Russia, with one marriage dissolved and another impossible, she will play the role of wanton society expects, but she will also needlessly coquette, so that she may test the force, the reliability of her beauty. Her need for beauty is insensate. Even before the break with Karenin, the visions in her head can only rarely be met in reality: Vronsky perceived must be raised to the level of the Vronsky of her imagination, while her son, whom she so fully, so physically loves, disappoints her expectations when she returns to Petersburg. But the figure of Karenin, as she meets him at the train, arouses not pity but repugnance: he is ugly and must be shut out. The effort to make life totally beautiful, like the effort to love and be loved unconditionally, causes her to miss something rather essential to life: the pain, compromise and occasional ugliness through which one may perceive a new and deeper joy. It is Kitty at the ball in Moscow, at the moment of Anna's rebirth, who recognizes that it is cruelty which heightens her enchantment, for Kitty is Anna's first victim: when Anna is born something in Kitty dies. And because all this rises from Moscow, where Anna is both mother and babe, where Vronsky is both father and servant, where Kitty is anxious midwife, it is quite natural, quite fitting that Anna is not provided with a past.

But Anna is not only a woman without a past; she is a woman with very little *sense* of the past. The study of history is an occupation totally foreign to her; all her needs can be compressed into a single moment, but the moment can never be repeated. Through the microscope we observe the path of the amoeba. A mere blob, a species of microscopic jelly, it strikes forth for food, edging closer to its quarry. Systematically it flows outward, grasps the particle to itself, alters its shape to accommodate its victim and then moves on, one being again, though not precisely in the form we observed earlier. Each time it chooses to annex more food, it must also form its new self. Anna perceives experience in much this way: each moment is not only an opportunity to grasp for the totality of the other, to love or to be loved absolutely, it also *expresses the totality of all experience with the other and the totality of all knowledge of self.* Whatever came before has little bearing upon the present: all deeds, both good and bad, slip into nothingness as new deeds are perpetrated; all memories, both joyful and melancholy, pass into oblivion as the next crisis arrives. Time's succession takes on the character of slides replacing one another on a screen, slides which our host has neglected to place in any particular order, so that we soon abandon any hope of discerning a harmony in what we see, and find our continuity in the mere sequence of brilliant images upon the screen, and in the moment of darkness which precedes them. When Karenin returns to Petersburg, to the wife he hoped might die, Anna triumphantly heralds the death of the woman who once loved Vronsky. But all memory of Vronsky seems dead too; until it is time for him to come forward and receive Karenin's forgiveness he is ignored. Later, as the novel draws to its conclusion, it counts for little that Vronsky has stuck by Anna with dogged faithfulness; each new meeting demands a renewal of their vows, however false such renewal seems to Vronsky. Prior evidence cannot appease Anna's doubts; the testimony of the moment must be judged solely on its own merits. A brilliant example of the manner in which Anna isolates herself from the past occurs in the scene which follows Anna's meeting with her son, after her return from Europe. Anna fails to tell Vronsky of her intention to visit Seriozha, for she knows that he will not react as she does, that he lacks the strength of emotion she requires, the ability to fix upon the instant as singular, confined, divorced from all others. "Her suffering was the more poignant that she had to bear it in solitude. She could not and would not share it with Vronsky. She knew that to him, though he was the primary cause of her distress, the question of seeing her son would seem a matter of very little account. She knew that he would never be capable of appreciating all the depth of her anguish, and that his cool tone if the subject were mentioned would make her hate him. And she dreaded that more than anything else in the world and so she concealed from him everything related to her son." (Yet Vronsky cannot help noticing that something oppresses her and, cast into his own isolation, concerns himself with her new mood.) The meeting with her son calls forth the worst and best in Anna: she tells Seriozha what is required, that he must love the father with whom he remains, but she cannot hide her hatred, her sense of competition for Seriozha's attention and regard when she catches sight of Karenin himself. Returning to her hotel room, more shattered by the meeting than she had expected, she tries to conquer her loneliness. She first turns to Vronsky's child, her daughter, but there is no satisfaction there: little Annie remains perpetually at a distance from her mother; she is indigestible, she cannot be wholly absorbed, so that Anna, through her, may assume a new self. Instead Anna chooses to compare Seriozha at that age to her second child, not to revive the past but to reaffirm the despair, the bitterness of the present. Rummaging through her photographs she suddenly and quite unexpectedly comes across a likeness of Vronsky. Though heretofore she has forgotten his presence, his very existence, his image now looms forth to blot out the past. Initially, however, it is a photograph of her son she seeks to extricate.

> Her deft little hands, whose slender white fingers moved with a peculiar nervous energy that day, pulled at the corner of the photograph, but the photograph had caught somewhere, and she could not get it out. There was no paper-knife on the table, and so, pulling out the photograph that was next to it (it was one of Vronsky taken in Rome in a round hat and long hair), she used it to push out her son's photograph. "Yes, there he is!" she said, glancing at the portrait of Vronsky and suddenly remembering that he was the cause of her present misery. She had not once

thought of him all the morning. But now, coming all at once upon that manly, noble face, so familiar and so dear to her, she felt an unexpected surge of love for him.

"But where is he? How is it he leaves me alone in my misery?" she thought suddenly with a feeling of reproach, forgetting that she herself had kept from him everything concerning her son. She sent a message asking him to come to her immediately, and sat waiting with beating heart, rehearsing to herself the words in which she would tell him all about it, and the expressions of love with which he would comfort her. The servant returned with the answer that he had a visitor with him but that he would come immediately, and that he asked whether he might bring Prince Yashvin, who had just arrived in Petersburg. "He's not coming alone, and he hasn't seen me since dinner yesterday," she thought. "He'll be coming with Yashvin, so that I shan't be able to tell him everything." And all at once a strange idea crossed her mind: what if he had ceased to love her?

The slides flash rapidly and abruptly upon the screen, they unnerve us by their brightness, their disorder; even the arbitrary moments of darkness form no respite, for we know they deceive us, throw us off guard, so that we may be even more shaken by new emotion, new shock. All the love Anna has felt for her son thrusts itself upon Vronsky, but no good will be derived from this "unexpected surge." She must commit to his care the full strength of her affection, but he is not there, and it seems unlikely, once he has arrived, that he will be in a proper mood to receive the gift she offers. And so—new image blazing upon the screen—love shifts to reproach, almost to hatred, but—yet another flash of light and brilliant slide—hatred is inadmissible, it causes one to doubt not the force of one's own love, but the love of the other. Torn by despair, by fear, by the wavering conviction she has lost her beauty, she goes to the opera, endures public humiliation, and thereby earns the right to demand she be loved unconditionally.

The curious face time bears, in Anna's portion of the novel, accounts for the many cycles and repetitions that come to dominate her life. Against the three major events of the first part of the novel—Anna's joy in Moscow, the seduction scene and the childbirth scene, which she regards as mere prelude to her death—we may place Anna's new joy in Europe, another seduction scene, this time between Anna and her son, and, of course, Anna's opportunity to again manage her own death. Moreover the final scene of part 4, in which Vronsky returns to Anna's home for one last visit, in which he and Anna unexpectedly decide to flee to Europe, contains all components of the Vronsky-Anna relationship: their passion; Vronsky's easy reassurances (now that he has expunged his guilt through attempted suicide his composure returns); their tendency to regard their love as exclusive, permanent, when it has not been such in the past and will be less so in the future; their capacity for communicating emotion to one another; their refusal to deal seriously with matters which threaten later discord; their unusual willingness to sacrifice too much — Anna abandons her son, because she now lives totally in Vronsky, while Vronsky gives up his post in Tashkent; Anna's self-pity, her inclination to use death for dramatic effect; their conspiracy to ignore rather than despise Karenin. By the end of the novel, as Anna is drawn inexorably toward the train, toward personal disaster and a new roster of victims — Vronsky, Karenin, to some extent her son — the pattern is so clear it warrants little comment. Indeed, in the final pages of part 7 Anna fully recognizes the pattern herself, but she can do nothing to dislodge its inexorable force. As she turns her blinding searchlight upon her own affairs, she grimly perceives that she is dissatisfied, and there is no further way the hated and urgent thirst for absolute love, first awakened at the ball in Moscow, can now be appeased. Bayley, in *Tolstoy and the Novel*, feels Anna still holds doom in abeyance, remains alive to the possibility of reconciliation, renewed love, because he sees her successive moods as linked rather than separate; he does not recognize they are slides which flicker on and off the screen, ever more rapidly, and thus misconstrues the compulsive nature of her quest. No matter; *she* knows the pattern cannot be broken:

> "My love grows more and more passionate and selfish, while his is dying, and that is why we are drifting apart" she went on musing. "And there's no help for it. He is all in all to me, and I demand that he should give himself more and more entirely up to me. And he wants to get farther and farther away from me. . . . He says I am insanely jealous; but it is not true. I am not jealous, but unsatisfied."

No character in a novel, from first draft to final copy, was ever more transformed than Anna Karenina. Here she is as Tolstoy first imagines her:

> She was unattractive, with a low forehead, a short, almost snub nose, and she was too fat. She was so fat that if she had been a little more so, she would have been deformed. If it had not been for her thick black lashes, adorning her gray eyes, her thick black hair, beautifying her forehead, if it had not been for the harmony of her figure, the grace of her movements, like her brother's, and

her tiny hands and feet, she would have been ugly. But, despite the unattractiveness of her face, there was something in the good-natured smile on her lips that made one like her.

From the very beginning Tolstoy struggles with the problem of properly conveying to his reader that his heroine is both attractive and unpleasant. The idea of physical unattractiveness, near obesity, a low brow and snub nose, does not work satisfactorily, for it too obscures the appeal of her smile and her grace. And what will snare the shallow Vronsky we meet in the early chapters of the work? He is not accustomed to searching for deeper beauty beneath a repellent exterior. But once Tolstoy makes Anna beautiful, must we assume he then falls in love with his heroine, loses his way and starts anew? Might he not merely take those less sympathetic qualities he wishes to suggest and place them on a psychological rather than a physical plane (a step of great importance for the novel's development)? There is still much "one can like" in the final version of Anna: her beauty, her wit, that strength of character which long holds her private devils at bay. Because I have tried to show how dominant the unpleasant side of her nature is, and how early in the novel it appears, I do not mean to neglect those more familiar aspects of her character which inevitably call forth the reader's sympathy. She is in every sense unique. Or, to use the adjective Soviet critics most often apply to her, she is a "nezuariadnaia zhenshchina," and "exceptional woman." Yet such a strongly individual temperament is something Tolstoy comes increasingly to distrust, as he moves toward his late period. Soon all traits of character which foster self-distinction will be condemned, but even now being unique can become a very mixed blessing: it breathes new life, new force into Anna at the ball in Moscow, and then burdens her with more vitality, more power than she can handle; it takes the finest product her class can engender, a truly beautiful and intelligent woman, and guides her to self-destruction. Early in the novel, as Anna searches for Vronsky to inform him she has confessed the truth to her husband, she finds herself at Princess Betsy's, in the company of women who are also carrying on affairs. Betsy, noting her anxiety, warns her she is becoming too serious, urges her to avert her gaze from the "tragic side" of life. Anna's response is significant:

"How I wish I knew other people as I know myself!" said Anna gravely and thoughtfully. "Am I worse than others, or better? Worse, I think."

How much in character Anna remains! It would never occur to her to ask—am I the same?

Anna Karenina: The Two Novels

Edward Wasiolek

Anna Karenina is two novels, Anna's and Levin's. The novel about Kitty and Levin's love is a familiar cartography, populated with people, situations, and values that we have met before. We are not surprised that the peasants resist Levin's attempts at agricultural reform, that conscious goodness such as Mme Stahl's will be disapproved, that the abstract intellectualism of Koznyshev, especially when it is used in the service of the public good, will be caricatured, and that true love will have something to do with bearing and bringing up children. Levin's novel has a pastoral quality, not unlike some of the scenes in *War and Peace*. The mowing scene reminds us of the hunt scene in *War and Peace*; like the hunt scene it celebrates mysterious self-absorption in immediate reality and the at-one-ness with others by way of that self-absorption. Levin's novel is a continuation of Tolstoy's art and a reaffirmation of his vision. The novel about Anna and Vronsky's love is something we have not met before in Tolstoy's work. Anna and the destructive passions that she embodies are enigmatic. Her love is an eruption of something almost demonic into the calm world of Tolstoy. Her appearance at this juncture of Tolstoy's work and the persuasiveness with which she dominates the novel comes from something unsettling in Tolstoy's horizon — something he was loath to confront.

Anna Karenina was written at a time when Tolstoy was going through a series of personal crises. There were three deaths in his family in the early 1870s; there was the feel of death at Arzamas; and there was the fact that he was in his middle years with all the reassessment and changed consciousness

From *Tolstoy's Major Fiction*. © 1978 by the University of Chicago. University of Chicago Press, 1978.

that the diminution of sensuous vitality brings. We know from his letters and diaries that he found the writing of *Anna Karenina* difficult to sustain; he found the work unpleasant, he was impatient to finish it, and he considered the end product to be repulsive. All the evidence seems to indicate that he was writing something that went against the grain of his conscious beliefs but which was nevertheless true. It was about this time that he stated in a letter to Strakhov (his close friend and a sympathetic critic) about *Anna Karenina* that it was impossible to lie in art without destroying the art. He may have told the truth in *Anna Karenina*, but he didn't like the truth. What appalled him about Anna's fate and what appalls us in its reading is the change that occurs in her person. She changes from a beautiful, warm person to one who becomes increasingly querulous, petty, and vicious. We are so moved by compassion for her suffering that we tend to overlook the fund of sheer nastiness in her by the end of the novel. Something in the love she bears Vronsky turns her from life to death and from love to hate. It is this something that constitutes the chief problem for explication in the novel. And it was this something that constituted a threat to everything that Tolstoy had believed up to this point.

Tolstoy had, of course, depicted love and physical passion in the works before *Anna Karenina*: there are seductions, romantic flights, and even irrational actions following on the impulses of physical passion. But they are treated lightly, as if whatever interference they posed in the good life could be easily disposed of. Masha in *Family Happiness* is estranged from her husband by the unnatural life she leads in the city. Among the banalities she experiences and finally discerns is the banality of romantic love, but no tragic consequences ensue; she feels only repulsion for the passionate Italian and ends up wiser and happier in the embraces of her middle-aged husband. The seduction of the mother and the near seduction of the daughter in *The Two Hussars* are both trivial and foolish—in different ways—and both are treated as escapades rather than personal crises. Indeed, the sex is incidental. The important point is the depiction of the virtues of one generation and the decay of those virtues in another generation. Even in *War and Peace* Tolstoy shows no consciousness of the destructive consequences of passion. Natasha's head is turned by Anatole, and she suffers disgrace; but time and the ministrations to the needs of others bring her to "natural" health and the dissipation of further romantic fantasies. Tolstoy depicts Natasha's love for Anatole as momentary foolishness, not as a tormenting part of her makeup. Physical passion and the temporary derangements of orderly life that it entails are treated in the early works as "errors" that experience, proper conditions, and the counsel of others correct. Princess Ellen and the coarse sensuality she embodies would seem to be an exception. But that is precisely what she is, an exception—an evil, coarse, very stupid woman who has little place in Tolstoy's conception life. He makes his nod to the existence of such creatures, showing his impatience with her by the sudden, unmotivated way in which he eliminates her from the novel and from his world.

There is no indication in Tolstoy's early works that a woman who lived in essentially beneficent conditions and one that was warm, intelligent, vital, sincere, and honest could be carried away by physical passion to the point of sacrificing her reputation, peace of mind, son, and even her life for the satisfaction of that passion. Tolstoy made his peace with the Betsy Tverskoys and Liza Merkalovs before *Anna Karenina*, but Anna herself was something new. Significantly, the early drafts of *Anna Karenina* show her to be a foolish, coarse woman. It is only reluctantly that Tolstoy comes to give her the redeeming moral traits that loom so large in the novel and which provoke so powerfully our sympathy. Yet it is as if in writing *Anna Karenina* Tolstoy perceived, as he had not done before, the full force of physical passion. Before she is carried away by her passion for Vronsky, Anna has been able to preserve her integrity in a corrupt society. Indeed, her passion is expressly differentiated from the banal passions of others in society, indicating that it is of a different order. If this is so, then nature itself, uncorrupted by false education, does not—contrary to what Tolstoy had long believed—automatically assure true forms of feeling. It appears, then, that it is not bad conditions that create false passion, but passion that creates false conditions. It is only after she is swept away by physical passion that the "unnatural" forms invade her life; that she flirts, lives abroad, exposes herself to foreign influences, disregards her maternal duties, uses birth control, and becomes dishonest, hypocritical, evasive, insensitive, and ugly in character. The very things that in other works would have explained why she had been swept away by physical passion become themselves the consequences and not the causes of the passion.

If then Anna's fate has not been caused by the corrupting influences around her, then the physical passion must have another source. But if the physical passion and its destructive attributes are something innate, something given, then they must be something in the order of nature. If this is so, then much of Tolstoy's edifice comes crashing down. It will not be enough to peel off the leaves of the onion to find the magic core; the core itself may be rotten. Tolstoy in the writing of *Anna Karenina* is at the point of a truly tragic stance, the acknowledgment that evil exists and is inextirpable from human nature. Up to this point Tolstoy had been an optimistic writer. No matter how much corruption and disorder he had found in human life, truth, happiness, and plenitude were in the order of things. It was only human stupidity and the cumulative codification of that stupidity in the conventions by which men lived that had clogged the pure springs of life. Is it any wonder, if the writing of *Anna Karenina* forced him to confront a situation that belied something essential in his world outlook, that he would feel a profound disgust with its writing and with art in general? He had, of course, almost from the beginning of his artistic career shown a suspicion of the ends of art and a distaste for his own part in furthering its ends. But never before had those feelings beset him with such intensity.

I am aware of course that, in the various explanations of why Anna degenerates as a person and commits suicide, the influence of a corrupt society is often put forth as a cause, as has been the tragic irreconcilability of love for both son and lover. But it is part of Tolstoy's magnificent art that he is able to engage our belief in what appear to be persuasive explanations, which nevertheless turn out to be untenable. Anna does not kill herself because God punishes her or because society punishes her, or because she cannot have both son and lover. She kills herself for reasons more obvious yet more mysterious than these. What makes her kill herself is the same force that at this point has such an unsettling and profound effect on Tolstoy's life and art.

The art is as different as the vision. One has the sense in reading *War and Peace* of watching different centers of a broad landscape come leisurely into focus. The sense of events uncoiling from prior events and the sense of character propelling events and hurrying to some predestined end is missing in *War and Peace*, indeed, in all the works written before *Anna Karenina*. The novel occupies less space; and its design is easier to grasp. This is why those of Jamesian and Flaubertian sensibility (as Percy Lubbock and F. R. Leavis) have preferred *Anna Karenina* to *War and Peace*. Tolstoy seems to have reacted to the less controllable aspects of Anna's fate by an increase in the control of his art. For there is more a conscious, even contrived use of structural niceties. As if in compensation for the enigma of the center, he increases his control of the periphery.

The control is apparent from the first pages in the relentless way in which Tolstoy pursues the developing love affair between Anna and Vronsky. The love affair from the first meeting at the train station to its physical consummation has a fateful character. Our first impression of Anna comes through Vronsky's reaction: Vronsky is compelled by some magnetism to take another look at her when she gets out of the train in Moscow, and Tolstoy's first description of her tells us why. Anna is described as someone in whom energy brims over into her brilliant eyes and smile. Vronsky notices the vitality in her being, even though she is regarded by her friends and her family as a woman comfortably settled in domestic life. Her mission to Moscow of domestic counseling tends to confirm the position she enjoys as someone wisely past the turbulence of life. Kitty, regarding her as an older confidant, draws upon her wisdom to help her with her romantic complications. We are confronted from the very beginning with two Annas: the settled matron past the turbulences of love, and the Anna of suppressed hunger for passion that attracts Vronsky at the first encounter. Tolstoy reinforces the "matronly aunt" image by various details. Dolly's children crowd about Anna, fingering her rings and the flounces of her dress. Anna responds to Kitty's excitement about the coming ball by an attitude of satiation with balls. The Anna who yearns for life beyond her role of wife, mother, and aunt is the hidden Anna who makes her first appearance at the ball.

Vronsky and Anna have covertly acknowledged an attraction at the railway station, but at the ball they come close to openly acknowledging their attraction for each other. Kitty, who has invariably pictured Anna in lilac, the color suited to a settled matron, is startled to see her dressed dramatically in a black dress set off by a single strand of pearls and a spray of pansies in her hair. The black dress with its sumptuous lace is something of an externalization of the luxuriant Anna that brims just below the surface of her settled manners and position. From their first meeting to the consummation of their love affair, Tolstoy will portray Anna as struggling against the "new" Anna that Vronsky has brought to the surface. Her protests are covert admissions. At the beginning of the ball, for example, Anna explains to Korsunsky, in response to his invitation to dance, that she tries to avoid dancing on such occasions. But as she finishes refusing Korsunky, Vronsky approaches, whereupon Anna changes her mind and offers her arms to dance with Korsunsky, failing even to acknowledge Vronsky's bow to her. Tolstoy, the consummate psychologist and artist, records by that inconsistency another detail in Anna's growing attachment to Vronsky. Korsunsky is her protection against the attraction she feels for Vronsky and the force of the rebuff to him is the measure of the need to protect herself against him. Anna will seek protection in the early stages wherever she can from what she feels for Vronsky. Her decision to return to Saint Petersburg earlier than she had planned—a decision she pointedly announces to Vronsky at the ball—is a form of protection by flight. She needs her husband, child, and settled life as quickly as possible.

Although the drama of passion is barely engaged in Moscow, Tolstoy seems to communicate that deep in Anna's heart it has already been concluded. For it is during her trip back to Saint Petersburg that Tolstoy celebrates Anna's "fall" into passion and the consequent transformation of her values.

I am referring to the scene on the train which symbolically records Anna's struggle between habit and passion and the victory of passion. It is a scene of intricately constructed parallelisms and barely concealed symbolizing. The scene—like the later one at the race where Vronsky breaks the horse Frou-Frou's back—begs to be dismantled. Tolstoy's intention is apparent, but the execution is, nevertheless, one of astonishing refinement. Once settled in her compartment, Anna wraps her feet in a plaid blanket and attempts to read an English novel of particular banality. The blanket is a protective detail and the novel a retreat into a make-believe world. But Anna is distracted from her reading by the bustle of people boarding the train and by various noises after the train has started. There is a tension between the make-believe, protective world in which she attempts to withdraw and the noises of the real world about her. She is distracted by the snow beating against the window pane, the sight of a muffled guard, and conversations about the terrible storm outside. In this context the storm is a symbol for the passion that rages in a deep level of Anna's being. Anna is separated from the storm by the window pane. Yet it almost touches her as it beats against the glass, and word of the raging storm is carried to her by the voices of other people. Her emotional ambivalence is accurately conveyed by the scene.

As she attempts to review what had passed in Moscow, a vague feeling of shame causes Anna to twist the knife in her hand. Trying to face the problem squarely, she concludes that she can find nothing to be ashamed of. But at the very point at which she exonerates herself from any shame in her relationship with Vronsky, the shame is intensified. Tolstoy is realistic enough to show us the limits of Anna's honesty. She attempts to face what is unpleasant but succeeds in avoiding it. The very vehemence with which she protests any possibility of other than ordinary relations between her and Vronsky convicts her.

As Anna turns to a form of unreality in her assessment of her own feeling, she returns to the fiction she is reading. But just as she cannot talk herself out of what she feels for Vronsky, so too she cannot force herself to be interested in the make-believe world of the silly English novel. Laying the book aside, she takes up the knife which she has been using to cut the pages of the book, touches the window pane with it, and then touches her cheek. The sensation of the cold knife causes her to laugh with delight. The knife may be taken as a detail signifying the destructive possibility of the passion, especially in a context that is manifestly sexual. The storm outside is communicated to Anna's cheeks by the instrument of passion; and what is communicated—the cold of the storm—relieves the flushed warmth of her cheeks and her passion. The storm outside relieves the heat inside. The imagery that follows this communication is almost coarsely sexual: Anna feels her nerves tighten as if on a screwing peg; her eyes open wider and wider; her fingers and nerves twitch; something within oppresses her breathing; shapes and sounds come to her in unaccustomed vividness. The symbolic acknowledgement of the claims of passion in her life seem to effect a transformation in her perception of the world. She does not know whether the train is going forward or backward; whether Annushka is her servant or a stranger; whether a fur coat on the arm of the chair is a fur coat or a beast. And most of all she does not know who she is: "Myself or another woman?" In effect a new woman has arisen within her and has been acknowledged by her—a division that is pursued to the bitter final days in which she commits suicide. It remains only for Anna to shake off symbolically the protective wraps of her former life and to go out boldly into the storm that is raging outside and inside her. In effect this is just what she does: she slips off her plaid and her cape, and the wind and snow burst into her compartment as an attendant comes in to look at the thermometer. As the train stops, there is a fearful clanging and shrieking, as if someone were being torn to pieces, and the room fills with a blinding dazzle of red fire. Anna feels as if she is sinking down; yet the sensation is not terrible but delightful. She goes out into the raging storm in search of relief from the heat of the compartment.

If the snow storm and the life outside the warm compartment symbolize the turbulence of passion, then Anna has moved ineluctably in this scene toward the acknowledgment of passion. Through the snow on the window pane, the communication of the cold to her cheek by the knife, the bursting in of snow and cold into her compartment, she is led finally to what seems to be a conscious and willed decision to go out boldly into the storm. It remains only that she meet the object of her passion. And this is what happens. Outside Anna takes deep breaths; the chill of the air relieves the heat of the passion within. As she turns to go back into the carriage, she meets Vronsky. At the moment that Vronsky looks passionately into Anna's face and her face registers joy and pride in her power, the snow storm becomes more violent than ever, sending snow flying from the carriage roofs and tearing off some clanking iron from a roof. The scene is a masterpiece of constructed symbolic detail. There seems little doubt that Tolstoy intended the storm and its attributes to stand for the passion that Anna craves and yet fears, and intended the entire scene to record the unconscious and barely conscious transubstantiation of Anna's attitudes.

Although, on the journey, Anna acknowledges symbolically the claims of passion upon her being, she does not cease to struggle against what her heart has acknowledged. On her first day home she plays the dutiful wife.

She does not go out; she waits for her husband to come home from his official duties; and when he returns, she forces herself to listen to an account of his brilliant official exploits. But her efforts do little to change what she feels. She has to fight a feeling of aversion for him—to argue herself into believing he is a good husband. She continues, too, to deny that she has any reason to feel guilty about what happened between her and Vronsky. Tolstoy gives us a little scene that illustrates how subtly Anna evades her true feelings. She unaccountably loses her temper at a dressmaker who has failed to have two dresses altered during her absence. Immediately after this uncharacteristic display, Anna once again goes over the events of her visit to Moscow, so as to assure herself that she had done nothing wrong in her relations with Vronsky. Once again she exonerates herself by convincing herself that her meeting with Vronsky was simply one of the trivial events of fashionable life. What does the display of temper with the dressmaker have to do with her self-exoneration? There is no doubt that Tolstoy wants these scenes connected, for not only do they follow each other, but Anna feels ashamed of herself after losing her temper as well as after exonerating herself. The shame is the tie. Anna has vented on the dressmaker the anger she feels toward herself and perhaps toward Vronsky. She displaces the shame she feels onto a trivial situation and another person. In effect she trivializes the shame as a way of protecting herself. It is in keeping with this form of evasion that Anna should go into the nursery to see her son after losing her temper. She spends the evening with him and puts him to bed. By her elaborate drama she protects herself against conscious acknowledgment of the true cause of her shame, but cannot annihilate the shame. The shame and guilt remain even though Anna attempts to relieve them by retreating to the habitual pattern of the guiltless mother.

With time, the defenses prove too weak and the attractions too strong. Anna's protests become weaker, her duplicities fewer, her desire more open. She chooses to move in Betsy Tverskoy's circle, which she had not frequented before because she knew she would meet Vronsky there. At one gathering at Betsy's, Anna and Vronsky become so absorbed in each other that they violate decorum. It is this violation that alerts Karenin. Karenin has taken no notice of Anna's growing intimacy with Vronsky until it has become a social impropriety and is reflected in the faces of others. Karenin's perception of Anna will always be mediated by group perception. He does not see Anna; he sees her indiscretion. Sensitivity to society, not to Anna, leads him to concern himself with Anna's behavior. Having perceived the attachment to Vronsky in conventional terms, later that evening he reminds her of her duty in conventional terms—of her duties to God and to the sacrament of marriage. This scene is often cited as evidence of Karenin's sensitivities and basic decentness. Yet it can be so read only if one shares the conventionalities Karenin lives by. Tolstoy is surely not presenting it that way. Karenin uses the general postulates of religion as justification of himself and as criticism of Anna, and most of all he uses them as a way of relieving himself of personal responsibility to Anna. He uses the Christian truths as he does administrative regulations. The scene is another instance of what Tolstoy has always been against: the generalizing of emotions and the consequent impersonalizing of them. Karenin does not see Anna the person, nor does he consult his own feelings or hers. He sees a generalized and official wife and mother, and he consults a system of ready-made values. The new Anna who has come into being on the train pretends to be ignorant of what he is saying and is unmoved by his counsel. She has lived by Karenin's rules and convictions, but Vronsky and his love have brought a different Anna into being. Her feelings, it is clear, have been severely repressed in her marriage with Karenin. It is natural that the repressed feelings should both frighten and attract her, as well as disorient her behavior. She is invaded by impulses which have not been directed by habit or reason. It is no wonder that they have the effect of creating another Anna. The presence of that other Anna is shown in this scene in her imperviousness to Karenin's appeal to the standards she has lived by, as well as by the enigmatic, frivolous, and elusive responses to his appeals. The new Anna and her old love are caught in the magnificent scene that brings the chapter to a close. As Karenin snores at her side, Anna stares, her eyes glowing, into the darkness, whispering to herself that it is late, late. Her old life is caught in the image of Karenin asleep by her side; the image of her new life is symbolized in the demonic glowing of her eyes in the darkness. There is both vitality and portent in the image. The glowing eyes are environed by darkness. It is too late for Karenin's counsel, but it is also too late for a great number of things. One will remember that when Anna throws herself under the train, Tolstoy takes us back to this scene, for the light that glows here in the darkness is extinguished by a huge, remorseless, impersonal force.

What Vronsky has pursued and what Anna has desired but dreaded, finally takes place, in one of the great seduction scenes of world literature. Matthew Arnold was right that Tolstoy pays no tribute to the Goddess of Lubricity. It is a scene not of titillation but of torment. What is dramatized is not passion but the effects of passion: the terrible significance of the act for Anna and the frightened helplessness and astonishment of Vronsky. Vronsky stands over Anna with trembling jaw, and Anna sits with her head bent down. She slips off the couch and would slip onto the floor if Vronsky did not hold her. The jaw is a reminder of the predatory character of Vronsky, and the trembling expresses his weakness. Not knowing how to calm Anna, he can only mutter ineffectually, "Anna, Anna, for pity's sake." But his voice is to no avail, for the louder he speaks, the lower Anna drops her proud head. She asks God to forgive her, but the words die on her lips when she looks at Vronsky. She is too honest to ask forgiveness when she has no intention of giving up a guilty love. She rises and says to Vronsky: "I have nothing but you. Remember that." Vronsky is all that she has and he will be too little. His words cannot calm her, nor can his arm support her. He has nothing to offer her but his passion, and this is all that he offers her now. What is caught here in gesture and word will obtain between them throughout the novel — Vronsky's helplessness, Anna's suffering, the divergent significance that each attributes to the act. Tolstoy compares the consummation to an act of murder. By that comparison he presages the destruction of Anna and implies that the love itself will lead her to death.

After the love is consummated, Vronsky encounters opposition from his family and friends and "suffers" from his irregular position. But neither Vronsky's love nor his suffering interfere with his appetite or his excitement about the coming horse race. We see him for the first time after the seduction scene on the day of the race and it is there that we have an opportunity to gauge the effect of the love on him. Tolstoy is careful to note that on the morning of the race Vronsky eats a beefsteak, that he had been paying attention to his diet, and that he is avoiding sweets and starches. There is room for many things in Vronsky in addition to whatever he feels for Anna. There is no room for anything else in Anna but the awesome emotions that have been aroused in her. We cannot conceive of Anna occupying herself with her figure and diet. We never see her eating; and no event could draw her away from her feeling for Vronsky and the guilt she feels toward her son. Anna gives everything to the love. Vronsky gives only what is proper and what he has to. He is sensitive to public opinion, to appearances; he is interested in other things. Anna is attentive to one thing only: her love for Vronsky and the painful situation attendant on that love.

When Vronsky sees Anna in the garden shortly before the race, he has an impulse to run to her but, glancing at the balcony in the belief that someone may be looking, checks his impulse. Tolstoy reminds us of the social check on Vronsky's love for Anna. In contrast, we first see Anna, after the seduction scene, alone in the garden with her forehead pressed against a cool watering can that she is clasping in her white hands. The face she raises to Vronsky is flushed and we can assume that she has pressed her forehead against the watering can to cool the fever inside her. The image is eloquent in its expression of Anna's emotional state. We know why Anna's face is flushed and why she is clasping the cool watering can. Vronsky does not. Seeing her flushed face, he asks her if she is ill. The question is a measure of his insensitivity. When he asks her what she is thinking of, Anna answers with heartrending simplicity, "Always of the same thing." Vronsky has been thinking of his diet, his mother, the remarks of his friends, his honor, the race, and Anna. But Anna has been thinking only of Vronsky and their love.

Since Vronsky is unequal to the passion and love that he has unleashed in Anna, the question must arise why Anna has fallen in love with someone so incapable of responding to her passion. Matthew Arnold was astonished that Anna should have been so irretrievably carried away by such a destructive passion, and that she should have been attracted to someone as unprepossessing as Vronsky. A case can be made for Vronsky, however. By every conventional standard he does act honorably. He gives up his ambitions, permits himself to be excluded from the society he obviously enjoys, and alienates himself from his family, friends, and social milieu. He is willing to marry Anna, fight a duel for her, and leave Russia for her. He is, in short, willing to do everything that she demands. His desire to regularize his position and to have his child bear his name are understandable wishes by humane as well as social criteria. In the closing pages of the book he is a man victimized. Anna tortures him with her moods, her irrational demands, her baseless jealousies; she attributes false motives to him and punishes him repeatedly. He seems to be a model of understanding. By the usual standards, Vronsky, it would seem, acts more honorably than Anna has done. Yet most of us are on Anna's rather than Vronsky's side throughout the novel, and the reason we are so is one of the magic touches of Tolstoy's art. Giving everything to a destructive passion may not be in the eyes of many a sign of health. Vronsky is a social animal, and in the depths of his feelings he is not much different from Stiva Oblonsky. One can even argue that Stiva carries off his "passions" with a certain childish innocence; that one of his functions in the novel is to provide us with an alternative to Anna's searing, fateful reaction to life. Tolstoy, it is clear, satirizes Stiva, as he does Vronsky for the most part. But there is just enough of truth in the characters of both men to create some ambiguity about how reprehensible their actions are.

Our sympathy for Anna comes clearly from the suffering she undergoes, not from some superiority of character or love. The notion of some critics that her love is better than Vronsky's because it is more intense is a romantic notion which disregards how destructive her passion is. There is nothing pretty about Anna near the end of the novel and nothing admirable about the love. If Vronsky cannot satisfy her demands, it is because they are not satisfiable. He is to be sure in many respects a superficial person. Like Karenin's, his passions are small, but he is no scoundrel because he cannot satisfy Anna's demands for love. No one could, for Anna would contrive to keep them unsatisfied. If Anna has chosen Vronsky to keep the love unsatisfied, then *she* has used *him*, and not he her. Anna, to be sure, is totally absorbed in Vronsky, whereas he is only conventionally attached to her. If in the course of the novel he gives more and more to the love, it is because Anna's demands carry him off to regions he would prefer to avoid but is too weak to resist. The horse race shows us how totally absorbed Anna is in Vronsky and how his attention is taken by things other than Anna. But the aftermath of the race begins to tell us, too, how that total absorption by Anna is a way of victimizing Vronsky.

Tolstoy's technique in the description of the race has something of the contrived quality that I have spoken of as a trait distinguishing the art of *Anna Karenina* from that of *War and Peace*. Tolstoy consciously—even obviously—pursues an analogy between Frou-Frou and Anna. The rough drafts to the novel show us that he does this deliberately, since the drafts make it even more explicit than the novel that he wants us to see Frou-Frou as a surrogate for Anna. The analogy is already apparent when Vronsky visits Frou-Frou's stable before going to see Anna at Peterhof. Frou-Frou has a clean-cut head, bright spirited eyes, which express energy and softness, and a strong neck, which Vronsky pats. The combination of energy, softness, and nervous excitement, as well as the strong neck are descriptive traits that Tolstoy has used before for Anna. The sexual relation of Vronsky to the horse and metaphorically to Anna is made clear: Vronsky pats the horse on its hindquarters, calls her "darling"; her excitement infects him so that his heart throbs, and he has the desire to move about and bite. The analogy between Anna and the horse is made even more explicit after Vronsky makes his blunder and breaks Frou-Frou's back. As the horse writhes on the ground like a bird that has been shot—the same image that Tolstoy will use of Anna in describing her misery at seeing Vronsky fall—Vronsky is described in these terms as he stands over Frou-Frou: "With a face hideous with passion, his lower jaw trembling, and his cheeks white, Vronsky kicked her with his heel in the stomach." The "lower jaw trembling," one must recall, was the descriptive detail Tolstoy used for Vronsky when he stood over Anna at the moment after the consummation of their love.

During the running of the race, Anna cannot stay within the bounds of decorum. She clutches her fan convulsively, her face is set and white, and she sees no one but Vronsky. When he falls, she moans and begins to flutter about like a caged bird. When other drivers fall, Anna pays no attention to them, a reminder perhaps of the selfish consequence of passionate absorption in one person, a consequence that is made evident by her insensitivity to her husband. She does not understand that Karenin's loquacity that day is an expression of his inner distress. Here as elsewhere Karenin is pictured as attentive to the public image, and inattentive to Anna as an individual person. When he arrives at the race track, for example, he has a hard time distinguishing Anna in the sea of muslin, ribbons, feathers, parasols, and flowers. The detail is both natural and metaphorical since Karenin has always a hard time "seeing" his wife. One must, however, feel some sympathy for what seems to be a genuine concern on his part not only for proprieties but also for Anna when she breaks down in the stands and he attempts to shield her from public disgrace. To be sure, he is once again concerned with appearances, but appearances and genuine concern cannot always be separated. Tolstoy will show us later that Karenin can in crisis feel through and beyond social forms. We must feel sympathy for him also when, in the carriage, Anna tells him that she is Vronsky's mistress, that she is in love with Vronsky and that she hates Karenin. The declaration is honest but brutal; Anna adds no qualification, no excuse, and makes no extenuation of the facts. She makes the declaration with total disregard for Karenin's feelings. The following morning, as she packs and considers running away, a letter from her husband arrives, filled with religious admonitions, informing her that he expects things to continue as they have done in the past. It is only then that Anna feels the full helplessness of her position: her love will be imprisoned by appearance, environed by deception, and reduced to the "regular" and banal affair that society countenances. This, I assume, is the reason that Tolstoy has her go to Betsy's garden party after receiving Karenin's letter. There she gazes at what she has been condemned to: the illicit relations carried on so gracefully by Liza Merkalov and Safo Shtolts.

What is already gnawing at her is the desperate fear—which becomes so prominent later on—that once her love is reduced to the level of gracious and well-regulated affairs, she will lose Vronsky. Vronsky's ambition lies just below the surface of his attraction for Anna, and in a very real sense he would be happy to have his position regularized. It is the irregularity, as he expresses it on several occasions, that he finds repugnant, whereas it is the regularity that Anna would find repugnant. His position once regularized, Vronsky would be free to pursue his political ambitions. In effect, Anna would end up being tied to another Karenin, a possibility signaled by the fact that both men have the same first name. It is to impress upon the reader this possibility that Tolstoy pursues an analogy between Karenin and Vronsky at this point in the novel. While Anna is torn with guilt and terror at the consequences she expects to ensue upon her confession to her husband of her love for Vronsky, neither lover nor husband share her intense feelings. The day after the race, Vronsky is engaged in doing his "lessive," that is, going over his accounts and taking care of his debts, and Karenin is busy with his program for the investigation of the native tribes. Both Karenin and Vronsky find the tenacity and intensity of Anna's passion to be an obstacle to their normal interests. Karenin is a very ambitious man, and Vronsky is touched very quickly by the possibility of spectacular political success, which his old acquaintance Serpukhovsky embodies and offers him. Like Karenin, Vronsky reacts to the intensity of Anna's feelings only by conventional words, values, and acts. When Anna tells Vronsky that she had told her husband everything, Vronsky reacts by picturing a duel in which he would exonerate his social honor. His solution to the impossible situation is as much of a social solution as is Karenin's arrangement by which appearances might be preserved. Anna wants something desperate, violent, decisive, something on the level of what she considers her act and love to be.

For a while she adopts the position that both Karenin and Vronsky force on her — a "respectable" position in which she agrees to Karenin's condition that she not receive Vronsky in their home. The position she is placed in soon begins to tell on her, however. When we see her after several months, she has changed for the worse, both physically and morally. She has grown stouter; her face is distorted with hatred; she has irrational fits of jealousy. One night on impulse, violating her promise to Karenin, she summons Vronsky to her house. Since Vronsky arrives just as Karenin is leaving, the men accidentally meet. The "accident" will appear to be less and less an accident in view of subsequent events. We can explain her fits of jealousy, her deliberate breaking of the rules she has agreed to, by the frustration of a woman living a love in conditions she finds degrading. But there is more to the accident. It is the first of a series of situations in which Anna will complicate her situation, provoking crises. From this first "accidental" complication to the agonizing last days, nothing distinguishes Anna's long, tragic deterioration more than this tendency to provoke complications, to reject what might be solutions to her terrible situation, to seek in its own way the death she finally embraces. If there is such a consistency to her actions, then the consistency tells us something about Anna's motivations. We can say, first, that Anna seeks such complications as a way of provoking Vronsky's attentions and to stem his drift away from her. It is a way of keeping the love and passion alive, although in a destructive way. The love weakens but the tie becomes tighter. The degeneration of Anna — the pitiful spectacle of a woman nourished on delusion, strife, punishment—comes from her efforts to keep the tie tight. Her self-destruction by suicide is the final attempt to keep the knot taut, even if it must be done by punishment, guilt, and self-destruction.

But the slide toward self-destruction is interrupted by Anna's near death in childbirth. Though Anna wishes to die in childbirth as a solution to her difficulties, she has not yet reached the point of actively seeking death. For a while the facts of childbirth and of near death bring her back to her basic self. Both she and Karenin grasp at something that is real in their relationship, and it is only Vronsky who comes off badly. As Karenin permits a better self to break through the layers of social control, Anna permits it to break through. There is no doubt that Karenin's feelings are genuine in the reconciliation scene, that his gratitude for what has been released in him and his consequent generosity to Anna and her lover are genuine. Karenin had earlier mouthed religious platitudes as he lectured Anna about her duties. Yet the religious joy he feels, in forgiveness, at what he thinks is her deathbed are true. The manner in which the emotion shows itself in Karenin is based on firm psychological evidence. Karenin is a well-disciplined person who has learned to control his emotions and who has become habituated to social control. Emotions for such a person are not easily expressed, except by way of permitted and ritualistic social forms, and when they do break through such social control, they are likely to be violent. It is only by such extra force that the repressive barrier can be broken. Needless to say, such an "explosion" will be at least temporarily disorienting. Karenin struggles with emotions he cannot control and which finally overcome him and his struggles. The blissful feeling that is released and which he tries to hold on to may, apart from its religious significance, be explained also as the relaxation of the struggle to keep his tensions unexpressed. It is perhaps significant that he sobs like a child, since the blissful emotion he feels at that point comes in part from sources deep in his being.

But Tolstoy shows how difficult it is for such genuine emotion to survive in the society that is portrayed in the novel, and how difficult it is to sustain that emotion in the face of momentum of past relations that reassert themselves once the extraordinary conditions are past. Once the danger of death is past, so that the normal relations can reassert themselves, Anna is still Anna and Karenin is still Karenin. Anna is still in love with Vronsky. Despite the gratitude she feels toward Karenin's generosity and despite her recognition of the spiritual heights Karenin had scaled, she still dislikes her husband. Karenin tries to hang on to the blissful feeling of forgiveness, as Anna tries to hold on to the feeling of gratitude toward her husband, but the force of society will insist that things be as they were before. Tolstoy tells us that besides the spiritual force controlling Karenin, there is yet another force, a brutal one which controls life. It is the force of society, that is, the expectation of others. Betsy is its embodiment: in Betsy's presence Karenin cracks his knuckles, bows stiffly, becomes cold and rigid; in Betsy's presence Anna begins to hate her husband again. After Betsy leaves, Anna cannot wait to get rid of Karenin; she tells Stiva Oblonsky that she hates him for his virtues. Karenin, confused and dismayed before Anna's irritation with him, is nevertheless willing to accede to anything that she might desire. He is willing to give her a divorce and her child as well, or to keep her as wife and let her keep her lover. His statement that he is willing to accede to everything means that he is willing to give her a divorce and her child too. Anna rejects all these offers, even while acknowledging his generosity. *Anna doesn't want a divorce*; *Anna wants Vronsky*. This statement may appear to be a contradiction, since quite obviously Anna will have Vronsky if she becomes divorced and marries him. But she does not want what the divorce will bring; she must know on some level that such "having" will no longer be the same "having." She goes abroad with Vronsky without a divorce and without her son, her only explanation being that she could not take advantage of Karenin's magnanimity.

The most persuasive and most commonly accepted explanations of Anna's motives and sufferings have to do with the irreconcilable love she feels for son and lover and the impossibility of having both. Yet at the point of her near death and Karenin's magnanimity she could have had both. Her reasoning that she did not want to take advantage of Karenin's magnanimity is evasive reasoning. She is not above hurting Karenin and, indeed, hurts him now, for by not accepting what his forgiving heart offers, she rejects him once again. *Anna does not want the son*, or, perhaps more accurately, she does not want the son if it means losing Vronsky; a regularized position in which she would be once again wife and mother would mean losing Vronsky. Tolstoy makes all this quite clear in what he tells us about Anna's feelings when she is in Italy with Vronsky. In Italy, where she has her lover but not her son, she has never been happier. When she made the rupture with her husband to leave with Vronsky, she justified her causing grief to Karenin by telling herself that she too would suffer in being separated from her son. But Tolstoy tells us that however Anna meant to suffer, she is not suffering, and he is careful to tell us that she does not even miss Seryozha. This is not to suggest that Anna does not love her son. Still, the irreconcilable conflict between love for the son and lover may be a simplification of Anna's motivations. One can dismiss her happiness in Italy and lack of yearning for her son as the temporary consequences of novelty and first feelings of delight in living with Vronsky. But other things lead one to see Anna's love for Vronsky as all-consuming and her love for her son as less powerful and perhaps even at times a pretext to provoke the love of Vronsky. It would be consistent with Tolstoy's views that a destructive passion would weaken the ties of motherhood. There is, finally, Anna's admission to herself on the last day of her life, while she struggles to understand what is happening to her, that she had not loved her son as long as her love for Vronsky was fulfilling. The passage is important enough to quote and to point out a serious translating error on the part of Garnett, who renders the passage to mean something significantly different from what it is saying: " 'Seryozha?' she thought. 'I thought, too, that I loved him, and used to be touched by my own tenderness. But I have lived without him, I gave him up for another love, and did not regret the exchange till that love was satisfied.' " The word "till" (*poka*) in this construction, should be "while."

Anna can live without her son and she can live quite happily also without society, as the sojourn in Italy shows. For many critics an unjust society is the cause of Anna's misery. There is every indication in the novel, however, that social conditions, whatever their form, are essentially irrelevant to Anna's misery. If Anna lived in a society that permitted love to flourish without the hypocrisy of her particular society, would she too flourish? I do not think so. Such easy love would probably be a greater threat to Anna than the constraints of her society. If she fears that Vronsky will cool toward her — and there is considerable evidence that she does — then it is the constraints of society that work to her favor, as a permissive society would not. Vronsky does have a social conscience even if he lacks a moral conscience. Feeling the "irregularity" of his relationship with Anna, he suffers from it, both for himself and for Anna. The love between Anna and Vronsky earns social opprobrium because it violates decorum. If Vronsky feels considerable discomfort because of social rejection, Anna too, it would seem, incurs considerable suffering through such rejection. But there is evidence that Anna needs a rejecting society — even its insults and cruelties. There is a very revealing scene after her return to Russia from Italy that underscores this need. Anna insists on going to the opera in a low-cut dress with the Princess Oblonsky, a person of doubtful reputation. By going out openly in society when her cohabitation with Vronsky is known, she exposes herself to public humiliation. Vronsky, horrified by Anna's intention, is astonished at her inability to understand what she is doing. Anna does understand, of course, but she purposely misunderstands. She knows that she is throwing down the gauntlet to society. Yet Anna wants to be humiliated, cut off from society, because by so doing she will also cut Vronsky off from society. There is no hint that Vronsky understands the price that she is willing to make him pay in order to have him as she wants him. Vronsky's reflexes are always social. Part of his "tragedy" is that he seldom understands Anna: He knows neither what she is doing to herself nor what she is doing to him.

Part of his "tragedy" is that he seldom understands Anna: He knows neither what she is doing to herself nor what she is doing to him.

Fearing the loss of Vronsky's love more than anything else, Anna sees social respectability as a threat to that love. After she is insulted by Madame Kartasov, she blames Vronsky for what has happened. In a sense she is right. He had with his love brought into being an Anna that he could not satisfy; because he cannot satisfy that love, Anna is driven to ever more extreme measures to provoke his love. She will take his love in any form that he will give it, but she will not take his indifference. After a terrible fight about the Kartasov incident, Vronsky calms Anna by trite asseverations of love, which Anna drinks in with shameless thirst. She will do what is necessary to tie Vronsky to her. Her tireless ingenuity, whatever form it takes, has but one end. It becomes ever clearer that Anna's enigmatic and increasingly desperate actions may have little to do with the loss of her son and social rejection but very much to do with a dread of losing Vronsky.

When Dolly visits Anna and Vronsky's country estate, she finds an Anna who devotes herself completely to Vronsky's interests. Anna spends a great deal of time making herself attractive to him; she reads on every subject that interests Vronsky; she interests herself in Vronsky's agricultural activities and in the hospital he is building. She lives for him, Dolly notices, and not for the child Annie. When they visit the nursery, Anna has trouble finding one the the child's toys and seems unfamiliar with the surroundings. Anna also horrifies Dolly by stating that she has no intention of having more children, because pregnancy will make her less attractive to Vronsky. It would seem that she would extend such devotion to meet Vronsky's deeply felt desire for a divorce so that his child and other children might bear his name. Yet she has been so evasive on this point that Vronsky asks Dolly to bring up the subject. When Dolly does so, Anna says she doesn't want to talk about it, but adds in contradiction that she thinks about the divorce every day, and that Karenin will not give her a divorce because he is under the influence of the Countess Lydia Ivanovna. She claims finally that, even if Karenin did grant her a divorce, he would not permit her to have Seryozha. While Anna's remarks outwardly suggest that she would like a divorce but is convinced that the possibility is remote, they may also be taken as the answers of someone searching for reasons for avoiding a divorce. Her belief that Karenin will not grant her a divorce because he is under the influence of Countess Lydia Ivanovna is a mere supposition; and her statement that a divorce would be futile because Karenin will not grant her her son is beside the point, since she does not have her son in any case. Anna really does not want a divorce; her evasive replies are a sign that she does not want to face up to the real reason why.

Why, then, does she a short time later write for a divorce and accompany Vronsky to Moscow to wait upon Karenin's decision? To ask for a divorce does not, of course, mean that Anna wants one or expects to get one. It is no accident that she decides to take the step when the chances of concessions from Karenin are few, and when she feels Vronsky is falling out of love with her. Her decision to ask Karenin for a divorce is a stratagem to justify going with Vronsky to Moscow. He had announced to her that he would have to leave her for a while to take care of some business matters, and she had angrily insisted on accompanying him. When he coldly insists on going alone, she impulsively announces that she will write to Karenin for a divorce and, by that strategy, gains the right to accompany Vronsky. Anna will use any weapon she has to keep Vronsky close to her: the weapons of beauty, flirtations with other men, devotion to his interests, even hurt, humiliation, and guilt. Anna is not above, for example, ignoring a child or using it if it furthers her possessive claims on Vronsky. She ignores Annie shamelessly, yet uses her to summon Vronsky back from the provincial elections by falsely asserting that the child is seriously sick. She cannot flout Vronsky's desire to marry her and give a name to his child without endangering the tie between them. By taking steps to secure a divorce she commands Vronsky's gratitude and by taking the step when Karenin is likely to make no concessions, she can reasonably hope to keep Vronsky separated from the public acceptance he so devoutly desires.

During their stay in Moscow, Anna flirts shamelessly with every man she meets, and her relations with Vronsky worsen. The strife that had entered their lives occasionally and which was always assuaged by Vronsky's embraces now becomes unrelenting. Anna seems to lie in wait for pretexts to hurt Vronsky; the moments of civility become fewer and briefer, the moments of reconciliation and expressed tenderness less and less satisfying. Anna by any conventional standard is responsible for the bitterness in their relations. She is convinced without rational cause that Vronsky's love has weakened, that he is interested in other women, that he is to blame for all her difficulties. She is irrational, punishing. In moments of lucidity she recognizes that he is not in love with anyone else, that he is still in love with her. We feel indignation at Anna's unreasonableness, but we feel great sympathy for her suffering. Most of all we feel shock to see the Anna who entered the pages of the novel exuding life, warmth, and sensitivity, now so cruelly transformed.

There are few scenes in world literature as painful to read as Anna's last day on earth. She is environed by emptiness. Within her is an abyss which she is helpless to fill. For her Vronsky alone can fill it, but he has left her—after the inevitable quarrel—to see his mother about business matters. As she waits for the word from the servant she had sent to summon Vronsky back, Anna attempts to fill the vacuum of time about her and in her. She cannot recognize herself in the mirror; she cannot remember whether or not she has done her hair. She can no longer coherently connect what she thinks with what she does and says. The world about her, including her own person, appears alien. The details that flash on the retina of her mind as she goes to see Dolly are, I believe, there to emphasize Anna's disconnectedness with the world about her. Life has become like a film that she watches but is not part of. She sees signs, people, dresses; someone bows to her; but none of what passes in front of her has any meaning to her. The visit to Dolly and the meeting with Kitty are as meaningless as everything else. Anna doesn't know why she has come or what to do. Tolstoy again projects Anna's inner stare onto the world outside her, and what she sees is ugly. Back home, not knowing why she has returned, Anna sets off to the railway station in an effort to catch Vronsky. On the way to the railway station she has a moment of lucidity: she understands that Vronsky will not deceive her, that he has no schemes about Princess Sorokin, that he is not in love with Kitty, that he will not leave her. The moment of lucidity sets off the darkness of the irrational impulses that are overwhelming her. In that moment, Anna understands that what is driving her to destruction has nothing to do with the many pretexts she has given herself. *She even admits that a divorce and the return of her son would not really change anything.* The feelings that Vronsky and she have for each other would not change, the shame would be the same, the contempt of other women would not diminish.

When Anna gets out at the provincial station and the coachman gives her a note from Vronsky nonchalantly saying he will be home at ten, Anna is engulfed with a feeling of desperate aimlessness. The world recedes from her. She exclaims, "My God, where am I to go?" Tolstoy could not have chosen a more appropriate setting in which to dramatize Anna's desperate lack of goal. The station itself is a background for people who are going somewhere. Anna is going nowhere and has nowhere to go. People rush past her, greet each other, embrace, pursue their destinations, reach out for each other. But Anna stands on the platform with nothing inside her or outside her; she stands on the edge of her being. It is then that she sees the approach of a heavy freight train. The platform shakes, reflecting physically the dizziness Anna feels. Tolstoy increases the tension: as Anna tries to fing herself under the wheels of the first car, she is held back by the effort to get rid of the red bag she is carrying. On her second try, she succeeds, and the candle which had illuminated her brief life is extinguished forever.

Why does Anna kill herself? The question asks why Anna degenerated from the life-loving, generous and humane person we first meet to the tormented, punishing, strife-ridden and strife-giving person she becomes at the end. One will want to exonerate Anna—to blame society, her husband, Vronsky, and surely to blame the conditions of her love. Good reasons can be found to exonerate her; Tolstoy gives us many. But although he loves Anna and weeps for her, Tolstoy is convinced that she is wrong and that the love she bears for Vronsky is wrong. To show that she is wrong he gives us a picture of the right kind of love in Kitty and Levin's love. The contrast between those two loves embraces the structure of the novel. Tolstoy has worked out the contrast in a deliberate way. While Anna is falling in love with Vronsky, Levin is being rejected by Kitty. When Kitty and Levin are falling in love, Anna is on her deathbed, attempting to reconcile herself to Karenin, struggling to give up Vronsky. As Anna and Vronsky leave Russia to begin their restless and aimless travels, Kitty and Levin are married. When Anna and Vronsky return to Moscow to make one desperate attempt to get a divorce and resolve their situation, Kitty is having a baby, finding new bonds of love and companionship with Levin. When Anna kills herself, Levin finds the secret of life in the words of an ignorant peasant. By and large the novel describes the deterioration of Anna and Vronsky's love and the growth toward maturity of Kitty and Levin's love. Both couples face some of the same situations, but the situations separate Anna and Vronsky and they bring Kitty and Levin together. Kitty, like Anna, experiences irrational outbursts of jealousy; like Anna, she feels unloved at times. Levin, like Vronsky, feels put upon by the demands of his beloved. Yet, while jealous outbursts increase the strife between Vronsky and Anna, they give Levin insight into the complexities of Kitty's soul. After Levin returns late and tells Kitty that he has been drinking at the club with Oblonsky and Vronsky and has met Anna, Kitty is convinced irrationally that her husband is in love with Anna. But the assurances of Levin assure Kitty, and the assurances of Vronsky that he is not in love with Princess Sorokin do not assure Anna. Later that night, when Kitty begins her labor, one of the important bonds between the couple becomes manifest.

To account for the difference between Kitty and Levin's "right" love, and Anna and Vronsky's "wrong" love, one may say that the former is "natural" and the latter "unnatural." But it is not so easy to say why one is natural and the other is unnatural. The good marriage for Tolstoy is free of the vanities of social life, fixed in mutual obligation of practical work, characterized by devotion of the partners to each other; most of all it is based on the birth and rearing of children. Levin and Kitty's union fulfills, or at least comes to fulfill, all of these conditions. But in large measure so does the union of Vronsky and Anna. They are surely devoted to each other, at least before the union begins to sour; Anna has a contempt for society and Vronsky comes to say that he has; they have a child; and for a time at least they are both engaged in practical work—Vronsky, like Levin, with the circumstances of agricultural work, and Anna in helping him in his work. Yet each of these conditions comes to separate them rather than to unite them. Some incalculable element converts some of the same things into a warm, growing relationship for Kitty and Levin, and some incalculable element converts the love of Anna and Vronsky into a destructive, humiliating relationship. Kitty and Levin's love ends, of course, in marriage and enjoys the approval of the society about them. There can be no doubt that the illicit relationship makes the love of Anna and Vronsky harder to maintain. But it is inconceivable that the legality of the one and the illegality of the other should explain the rightness and wrongness of the loves. Tolstoy makes it amply clear that he has nothing but contempt for much of what is approved by society. It is equally clear in his description of Anna's love that something deeper than the violation of convention lies at the basis of the destruction which overcomes that love.

This incalculable element cannot be the cruelty of the society in which Anna lives, nor the condition of irreconcilable love of son and lover, for the reasons I have already explained. Even less can it be what the epigraph suggests: that Anna suffers because she has sinned. Karenin thinks about God, but Anna does not. During her last day on earth Anna does not think about society, divorce, sin, or her son; she thinks only about Vronsky and his lack of love for her. Her last words are: "I will punish him and escape from everyone and from myself." She kills herself, at least as she explains it to herself, in order to punish Vronsky. This is not the first time that the thought of death has been linked in her mind with punishing Vronsky. It is, in fact, a repeated refrain. At the time of the quarrel about when to leave for the country, she solaces her "horrible shame" with the thought of death: how, if she died, Vronsky would repent, pity her, love her, and suffer for her. She smiles with satisfaction at the thought of his feelings after she is dead. If she is killing herself in order to punish Vronsky, then the motive is in keeping with what she has been doing to him throughout the affair. Since the consummation of their love, she has been punishing him by her fitfulness, her refusal to get a divorce and regularize their position, her jealousy, as well as by direct taunt and insult. "Where love ends hate begins," she tells herself as she prepares to end her life on earth, implying by this a necessary transition from one to the other. If Anna cannot have Vronsky by love, she will have him by hate. Many of her irrational actions are explainable as attempts, pleas, strategems, by which to compel, if not Vronsky's love, at least his attention. If nothing else will turn Vronsky to her, perhaps the pain and guilt from her death will, if only in memory. All of this, while explaining why Anna acts and speaks as she does, does not explain why she would want to cling to Vronsky with such compulsive possessiveness. Nor does it explain why she hates herself as much as she hates Vronsky. For she is convinced that she is a shameful and corrupt woman. When, after the quarrel on the subject of when they should leave for the country, Vronsky comes to her tenderly and tells her that he is ready to go whenever she wants to, she cries out in tears, "Throw me over, get rid of me," for "I am a corrupt woman." Only the desperate, passionate caresses which she showers on him are able to still for a little while the hate she feels for herself. On the day before her suicide, after Vronsky's departure, she imagines his saying to her all the cruelest words that a coarse man would say. The next day, on her way to see Dolly, she catches herself in her thinking by noticing, "Again you want humiliation." The ugliness she sees around her on that day is surely the ugliness and hate she feels in herself.

The shame, as well as the deisre to punish Vronsky and herself, come for Tolstoy from the nature of the love itself. It is the love that is wrong, not Anna or Vronsky or Karenin or society. And what is wrong with the love, for Tolstoy, is that it is contaminated and corrupted by sexual passion, whereas Kitty and Levin's love is not so contaminated. Tolstoy insists rather coarsely on the physical basis of Anna's love. The imagery used to describe the suicide is sexual: the huge railway car throws Anna on her back; the peasant who appears at this point and who has appeared in her dreams is probably a symbol of the remorseless, impersonal power of sex. As he beats the iron, he pays no attention to her. In an early instance of the dream that she recounted to Vronsky, the bearded peasant (who mutters French phrases) runs into her bedroom. Vronsky too associates his dream of the peasant with the hideous things that he had to witness in conducting the visiting foreign prince about town. The last agonizing hours she spends on earth are also filled with sexual references. There is the explicit acknowledgment that she cannot live without Vronsky's caresses; she shudders with the imaginary physical caresses on her back as she stands in front of a mirror examining her hair. She sees the world about her as dirty, and such dirt is associated with shame and with the self-hate resulting from the slavery of sex. She reacts to children buying ice cream by the bitter acknowledgment that she has lived only for her dirty appetites, as do all people. On the train she mentally undresses a stout woman dressed in a bustle and finds her hideous.

It is the nature of physical passion that works for the destruction of

Anna and Vronsky's love, brings them to hatred of each other, brings Anna to hatred of herself, makes their relationship more and more spectral, breaks down the communication between them, brings them into a situation where they cannot speak frankly to each other, makes them avoid certain subjects, and forces them to surround themselves with other people so as to make each other's presence tolerable. Kitty and Levin's relationship, on the other hand, is free of passion: they argue, work together; they feel close and at moments drift apart; they love each other and the love grows and prospers, but there is no indication on the part of either that the body of each is in some way the basis of their closeness. Kitty and Levin's union is uncontaminated by sex. They draw closer to each other because they come to respect a certain distance; the constant refrain of Levin's understanding of Kitty is her difference from what he had imagined her to be. He comes to see and respect a center in Kitty different from his own and he permits her to work out her own relationship to children, work, the household, and people, just as she permits him his absorption in his agricultural theories and practice. The work of each is serious in a way that the activities of Anna and Vronsky are not. Vronsky's hospital, agricultural management, machinery, and painting strike us as pretexts; and Anna's care of the English children, her writing of a children's book and her absorption in agricultural books are patently pretexts. Anna herself recognizes this in her scorching analysis of her relationship with Vronsky on the last day of her life, when she calls their activities pastimes (*zabavy*). Vronsky never enjoys the kind of total absorption in work that Levin enjoys when he cuts hay with the peasants.

Tolstoy sees sex as a massive intrusion on a person's being and a ruthless obliteration of the sanctity of personhood. Both Anna and Vronsky feel coerced and manipulated by the other. The stronger Anna loves, the more she coerces and the more she alienates. The corrupting power of sex seems to be an extreme example of what Tolstoy has always been against: the attempt of the individual to make the world one's own and the consequent impoverishing and desiccating effect that such coercion has on the world about one. The truth he reaches in *War and Peace* consists of the consciousness of the plenitude of life that one attains when one gives up one's control of the world. The centers of being of others with all their radical uniqueness come into consciousness only when one permits them to so arise. The right love also, for Tolstoy, comes into being under the same conditions. And although it happens for Kitty and Levin, one cannot avoid the feeling that the love is there to assure Tolstoy that what he has believed in is still valid: that one can find wisdom, happiness, peace, fulfillment, no matter how powerfully Anna's story seems to argue the existence of something in nature that makes these things impossible.

Such an explanation of Anna's deterioration and death is consistent both with Tolstoy's view of life and with the course of Anna's actions in the novel. Anna's is a possessive love. Feeding on its possession, the love alienates or destroys what it attempts to possess. Tolstoy signals this in the seduction scene, when he compares the act of physical love to an act of murder; this is for him no idle conceit, for possessive love does kill what he considers to be the fount of a person's being—something sacrosanct, radically individual, belonging to no man but only to the self-in-God. Vronsky resents Anna's invasions of his personality, reacts unfavorably to her attempts to coerce him into undivided attention to her; yet his very resistance provokes Anna to demand more and more. The duel of control and resistance leads Anna to more and more hysterial attempts and to resentment too, because of his refusal to give himself entirely to her. Suicide thus becomes the final attempt to control his being by way of guilt. Tolstoy has built into the structure of the novel a fairly probable course for Anna's actions that is in keeping with his personal distaste for sexual love. He has in short been able to generalize what is personal and for many a bizarre view of sexual love, and to incorporate it into his general views about what desiccates life and what makes it flourish.

What is more, with his immense talent he has been able to dramatize the course of such a love so that it appears persuasive in its consequences. All this is Tolstoy's reading; yet it is not the only reading that the text will support. There is, of course, a presumptive validity to what the author has on some discernible level of structure led the reader to believe; yet the reader is not bound to accept—and, indeed, in some cases must not accept—the author's intentional structure as the definitive structure of the novel. I am talking about an intentionalism that one can discern in the novel, not one pronounced by the author in letter or diary. Wimsatt and Beardsley disposed of the latter some decades ago, but the "intentional fallacy" disposed of one kind of intentionalism and obscured another. The personal predilections, even eccentricities, shape the inner relations of the text in an inescapable way. The author's text is only one of many. Otherwise the text would be the prisoner of a special personality; no matter how great, it would still be limited and fixed in a special time. Anna's fate continues to provoke in us powerful feelings of compassion and mystery for reasons other than those Tolstoy has worked into the structure of the novel. Tolstoy has drawn a powerful portrait of a woman tortured and torturing, loving and hurting and being hurt. The portrait moves us as powerfully as it did Tolstoy's contemporaries, but for different reasons—reasons supported by structures in the text. Tolstoy's views on sex were already extreme at the time he wrote *Anna Karenina*; they are bizarre today. If Anna's terrible fate is the consequence of her sexual love and its evil nature, as Tolstoy would have us believe, and if this were the only explanation that the text could support, then I do not believe the novel would continue to move us as deeply as it does. There seems little doubt that in reading *Anna Karenina* we are in the presence of one of those great texts, the structure of which is multiple and which in its richness can support a great number—perhaps an inexhaustible number—of explanations.

The compulsive nature of Anna's love and the delusional nature of her mental life as the novel progresses would lead us, for example, to look for some psychoanalytic explanation of her motives. Anna is a driven person who becomes increasingly impervious to rational argument and objective evidence and increasingly incapable of discerning with reasonable accuracy the reality about her. It is some inner need that directs the course of her actions, feeding her delusions and distorting the reality about her. Tolstoy has instinctively perceived that Anna uses the reality about her to camouflage a hidden reality. He gives us what appear, but only appear, to be explanations of why she acts as she does: the cruel society, the irreconcilable love of son and lover, the social shame before her actions, the conscious guilt at having hurt her husband, the fear of being abandoned by Vronsky. But Tolstoy has signaled that in the end these are all pretexts or rationalizations for something else.

Tolstoy explains the delusions as consequences that proceed from the nature of sex, which he looks upon as destructive of the sanctity of being. Perhaps, but not necessarily. A consequence in one system of explanation may be cause in another. What is painfully apparent on the last days of Anna's life is that Anna's misery does not come from the threat of abandonment by Vronsky, but that the threat of abandonment is a consequence of some other cause. Anna courts abandonment by insulting Vronsky and pushing him to hate her. Although Vronsky is not involved with other women, Anna insistently and obsessively needs to feel that he is in love with someone else. Vronsky does not hate her or see her as a corrupt creature (as she repeatedly charges him with thinking), but Anna needs to feel that she is hateful and corrupt. Why does Anna want to be hurt? to feel humiliated? and why does she court and propel the very things she fears and loathes? If not from external causes, then from inner causes, and from drives that seem unmodifiable by external circumstances. Nothing is more obvious than the "trapped" nature of Anna's feelings. If these destructive drives are so deep and powerful, they can only come from early experiences.

We know nothing about what led her to marry Karenin, but we do know that Karenin is twenty years older than she, and that his whole manner is one of public and private authority. One of the elders of society, he is something of a father to Anna. If Anna feels abused by Karenin's emotionless relationship to her, we might entertain the hypothesis that some psychic need was being satisfied when she chose him for her husband. This hypothesis takes on some credence when we see that Vronsky, for whom Anna abandons Karenin, in many ways resembles her husband. From Vronsky too Anna suffers from the threat of abandonment, and from a coldness that she discerns in him and projects onto him. That Anna should have been swept away by someone as unprepossessing as Vronsky—which astonished Matthew Arnold—becomes less mysterious when one entertains the hypothesis that Vronsky may be precisely the kind of person Anna needs: that she has chosen someone who will not meet the demands of her love and someone who will—with good form and a sense of honor—abandon her for social and political standing.

What I am suggesting is that Anna neurotically chooses someone who will hurt her, that she courts the feeling of being unloved, and chooses a situation in which she will feel shamed and corrupt. It matters not a bit that her sense of abandonment and emotional abuse is in good measure imaginary. The delusional nature of her hurt signals to us how compulsive and unchangeable her needs are. The need to be abandoned and hurt and the need to feel corrupt and hateful must come from sources deep in her being and early in her upbringing. Though we know nothing about her childhood, we do know that the sense of corruption precedes rather than follows upon the self-destructive acts she engages in. We also have some hints in the text itself that the drama in its most painful stages is related to her childhood; at least elements of childhood feelings invade her reflections at certain moments. On the night before her suicide, Anna waits in her room like a petulant child for Vronsky's return and for proof of his love by a visit to her before going to bed. She waits like a child waiting to be tucked in for the night. On the morning of the day of the suicide she kisses her hand as a mother will do to a hurt child. When she commits suicide her last thought is of herself as a child. We know also from the text that Anna suffers from the delusion that Vronsky loves another woman, who, in the last days, becomes increasingly his mother. Vronsky's mother, who becomes the obstacle to their moving to the country, is for that moment at least the cause of Vronsky's abandonment of her. It takes only the mildest of displacements to shift the cause of being unloved and abandoned by Vronsky from Vronsky's mother to her own mother. And if Vronsky represents for Anna's psyche a repetition of Karenin and the paternal image, then Anna in her last delusional hours reenacts a drama of terrified child facing abandonment by the father because of the intervening and hateful mother.

Once one begins to reason in this vein, a host of statements, actions, and ruminations begin to develop in a way different from the way Anna's fate is usually explained — whatever the range and variety of explanations — and different too from the way I have explained Anna's motives. I am not suggesting that *Anna Karenina* is best read as a psychoanalytic drama, but I am suggesting that one of the reasons the novel escapes the constricting force of Tolstoy's bizarre views on sex lies in the fact that multiple novels can be constructed from the order of dramatic events given. This is to say that the author's intentionalism — however deeply we see it imbedded in the text itself, and whatever term we wish to use for such a presence, whether "implied" or "realized" author — has a limited control over what we read and should have a limited control over what we accept. The emotions we give to *Anna Karenina* come from sources in part different from those that feed Tolstoy's passion.

We have, of course, an obligation to discern what the author has put into his work, but it will do his work and him no credit to limit its power to the sometimes eccentric views of the author himself. If a great work is "universal" — and I think *Anna Karenina* is universal — then it expresses and escapes even the deepest recesses of the author's creative being. This study is devoted to tracing out the special "mythology" of Tolstoy's view of reality and man's proper relationship to it, as Tolstoy has confronted this relationship in his fictive hypotheses. But I believe that such a "mythology" or personally structured experience is something that we must displace if we are to bring the structure into reasonable alignment with our understandings. *Anna Karenina* is powerful evidence for the spiritual and emotional biography of Tolstoy at this juncture of his life, for it shows how mightily Tolstoy attempts to integrate his increasing aversion to sex into a structure of experience that he had formulated so beautifully and coherently in the early works, especially in *War and Peace*. It is because he has trouble integrating Anna into his structured world that so much of her escapes his understanding and control. Kitty and Levin's love is there to reassure us and especially Tolstoy himself that everything he believed in before *Anna Karenina* is still true. Tolstoy takes Levin to the fountain of truth again. But because it is a truth we have seen before it is less persuasive, especially when seen against Anna's fate.

The truth that Levin comes to is the truth that all the heroes of Tolstoy's novels come to: what Olenin glimpses and what Pierre and Natasha experience for a while, and what Karataev epitomizes: that one is in touch with reality when one empties oneself of wishes, desires, thoughts, plans, intentions. The world about one, incalculable in its movement and complexity, becomes one with oneself when one permits it to be. A good part of Levin's story, for example, has to do with plans and failures in his dogmatic attempts to bend life and people to his will. His plans are continually frustrated by the peasants, much as Pierre's reform intentions are sabotaged by the realities of peasant life. The peasants wreck Levin's machinery, disregard his instructions, steal his hay, and are uninterested in his reforms. They are like the recalcitrant element of life which refuses to give itself to the abstractions of Levin, as life had refused to give itself to the abstractions of Olenin, Prince Andrey, and most of Tolstoy's heroes up to his point. Levin comes to learn the most precious of Tolstoy's truths: that reality gives itself to one when one ceases efforts to possess it. Perhaps nowhere in the novel is this expressed more beautifully than in the "sacramental" scene of the hay mowing. In that scene Levin experiences, if only for a day, what the feel of reality is; and if the scene is no effective answer to the destructive impulses in people that Anna has introduced, Tolstoy's art is so great that one feels that it is an answer.

Levin's right relationship to the land and life is contrasted with his brother's wrong relationship. His brother Sergey Koznyshev has come to the country to relax. He comes to the country not to fill his being but to empty it. The beauty of the season and the imminence of the practical work of harvesting have absorbed all of Levin's sensibilities. He takes part only half-heartedly in the argument with his brother about the relative merits of working for the public good and working for one's own self-interest. Tolstoy, one might note in passing, is very much on Levin's side when he insists that the mainspring of action is self-interest, as he is on Andrey's side against Pierre in a similar scene in *War and Peace*. As in *War and Peace* he uses "self-interest" with no pejorative overtones. What he means by the term is living concretely, for one's immediate self rather than for an abstract self. It is the "public good" and abstractions of that kind that separate man from the immediate reality about him and conceal a predatory self-interest.

As Levin mows with the peasants, he forgets about the idle argument he has had with his brother. The mowing is real, and the argument appears unreal. Levin learns something on the day of the mowing that he had not learned from the book he was writing or from his plans to reform himself and the peasants. He learns that one does not understand the peasants and the land by conscious analysis but by becoming at one with the land and the peasants. The peasants he works with are not functions of his understanding; they are real people who work more skillfully than he and who have identities and centers just as he has. As the day goes on, his consciousness of what he is doing becomes progressively obliterated. With that obliteration Levin becomes at one with the scythe, the workers, and nature. At first he tires easily, but as he gives himself to the job, mowing with the same rhythm as does the older peasant, the job becomes effortless. When the work is going smoothly, Levin thinks of nothing, wishes for nothing, and hears nothing but the swish of the scythe. As soon as he becomes conscious of what he is doing and tries to do it better, the mowing becomes more difficult and the row is badly cut. We are confronted once again with the phenomenon that one's personal effort interferes with one's right relationship with the world. Levin "understands" the world about him when he is at one with it, and he is at one with it to the extent that he ceases to separate himself from it by thought, desire, and will.

Tolstoy expresses this unity of self and surrounding by some brilliant stylistic strokes. Levin takes a short nap after dinner—a tuft of grass for his pillow—and when he awakens the world is changed for him; he feels himself to be at one with the world about him, and the union of inner and outer is caught in the style itself. Tolstoy speaks of the "slanting trays of the evening sun" (*na vechernikh kosykh luchakh solntsa*). Since the Russian word for "slanting" (*kosoy*) is a homonym for the word scythe (*kosa*), the natural image of time is identified stylistically with the instrument of work "scythe." The river is described as gleaming at its bends like steel bands, so as to remind us again of the gleaming steel of the scythes and to suggest the unity of tool and the natural image of the river. The same verb "gleaming" (*blestet*) is used for river, meadow, and scythe. The tool and the world acted on are one, as are the action and the actor. As dusk falls, Levin loses sight of his fellow workers. Only the sounds of the men urging each other on, the clank and hiss of the scythes, the sound of the whetstones are heard, like some natural chorus. At the beginning of the day Levin had been very conscious of the names of the peasants and of their personalities, but at the end of the day only the common sound of the group united with nature in work remains in his consciousness. As the day progresses, he loses consciousness of himself as different from them. It is the immediacy of the work and of the common task that effects this. Tolstoy speaks of the work as "boiling" at this point (*rabota kipela*); the image is that of the mist coming from the meadows, uniting stylistically the work with the natural surroundings. Levin's sacramental moment consists in his temporary loss of concerns and cares of a world that goes beyond the immediate situation and the submergence of his being in collective work and in the immediate surroundings. Permitting the world and the peasants to be what they are, he has permitted himself to be what he is. For that day Levin does not feel himself as a "postponed" being, someone who has alienated himself in future Levins or in past Levins, or a Levin who is imprisoned in his conception of who he is or should be. He is a concrete being, who is at one with himself, those about him, and the physical world about him. Tolstoy not only states that nature, man, and his activity are one; he makes them one in image and word.

When Levin returns home, he finds that his brother Sergey has spent the entire day inside going over reviews of his work and studying miscellaneous papers. Sergey's only response to nature is to scold Levin for letting flies in. He attempts to dredge up the previous day's argument, but Levin is uninterested. He does not contest his brother's distinctions, and the whole problem seems trivial in comparison with the reality he has lived that day. Levin has been able to achieve the unity with the land and the peasants which he was not able to do by his plans for them. It is a good moment because Levin "follows" and does not "lead," permits himself to be and does not force himself to be. The communication between him and his brother Koznyshev is there by way of contrast between "false" communication and "true" communication. One is false because it consists only of words and ideas; the other is true because it consists of one's whole being uncoerced by the willed communication of words.

The mowing scene is something of a confirmation of the epiphany that Levin experiences near the end of the novel after all his searching for the truth. We will remember that Levin goes reeling down the road from the impact of a peasant's distinction between one peasant who lives for his stomach and another who lives for his soul. According to Levin's interpretation of this, "He said that one must live for one's own wants, that is, that one must not live for what we understand, what we are attracted by, what we desire, but must live for something incomprehensible, for God, whom no one can understand nor even define." Levin, it is to be noticed, interprets *nuzhdy* (needs or wants) by desire and the need to understand. Since these are presumably what keeps one from the truth, they are examples of the force that have kept Levin from the truth and have condemned Anna to live in falsity. Levin has been kept from the truth by his efforts to understand; Anna by living for her desires.

Despite the feel of reality of the hay-mowing scene and its undeniable beauty and expressiveness, one is left with the feeling that Anna has won the day, that all of Levin's searching and finding are insubstantial if they do not confront the destructive power that Tolstoy has located in Anna's physical passion. The Levin plot has something of an air of a fable, beautiful but remote, whereas Anna's plot has the air of pressing reality. When Anna and Levin meet briefly near the end of the novel, it is Anna that sweeps Levin temporarily into her orbit and not the other way around. He is captivated by her beauty and intelligence and thoroughly won over to sympathy for her difficult position. But Anna is untouched by Levin. When he leaves her presence, she ceases thinking about him. Levin lives in the secure, rationally dominated world Tolstoy had constructed before he discovered Anna, while Anna lives in a world ruled by demonic passions which, one is convinced, would sweep away any consideration of the wisdom that is embodied in Levin's life. Tolstoy bravely puts forth Levin's life as an alternative to the moral center of Anna's world, but he dares risk only the briefest of encounters between these two worlds.

After *Anna Karenina* and the ten-year hiatus in his creative work which followed upon his religious conversion, Tolstoy wrote principally only about two things: sex and death. The two were associated in his mind. Sex for him serves death, as it does in *Anna Karenina*, almost in eerie anticipation of the Marcusian interpretation of Freud, in which the sexual impulse is seen to be in the service of the death instinct. Tolstoy saw sexual passion as degrading, and destructive of man's spiritual self. Many of his works after the conversion, at the time of his renewed interest in creative writing, are campaigns against the corrupting attributes of sex, as *The Devil, Father Sergius* and *The Kreutzer Sonata* eloquently show.

The Kreutzer Sonata was to summarize Tolstoy's feelings of disgust with sex. Absent from this novel is the sympathy Tolstoy had felt for Anna in the grip of passion. The dogmatism and intractability always just under the surface of his views burst forth to bludgeon the reader. Love, or what the world called love, was for him not only stupid but degrading and repulsive. It was more than that: it destroyed everything human in people and in the end destroyed the people themselves. There are hints of this in *Anna Karenina*, though the compassion with which Tolstoy treats Anna's life mitigates what she does to herself. Anna is wrong and Levin is right; there can be no doubt about that; but even if wrong, she is still to be loved and pitied. In *The Kreutzer Sonata*, however, there are no such mitigations: those who give themselves to sex are lunatics and ugly, vicious people, and the world which encourages such love is ugly and vicious. Even in marriage, sex is repulsive and destructive. The point of the narrative of Pozdnyshev is to show how sexual love degrades a human being, thus arousing hostility to others and to himself. Pozdnyshev kills his wife not because she may have had an affair with Trukhachevski—whether she actually did is never made clear—but because he himself has slept with his wife. Those critics who have argued for or against the reality of Pozdnyshev's wife's fall have missed the point, for it really doesn't matter whether she fell or not. It is quite probable that the wife's fall is a product of Pozdnyshev's deranged imagination, but it is the immoral act of sexual relations with his wife that has brought him to such derangement.

The agitation Tolstoy felt about the question of sexual relations had its effect on the construction of the novel. Eager to spew forth the various arguments he has and has had about sexual relations, he fails to connect the diverse points, some of which are directly contradictory. He argues, for example, against the corrupting influence of society because of its view of sex; its hypocrisy, commercial exploitation of women and men, and the pervasive air of deception that it encourages. The argument against the way men and women are brought up in society would seem to indicate that these corruptions can be remedied and that a love other than that which obtains in society can be imagined and perhaps even established. Indeed, the old tradesman's defense of traditional views on marriage and the relations between men and women lead us to believe that there are better ways of arranging these things in society than those which are practiced. Yet in the end Tolstoy makes clear that sexual relations, whatever their form, are destructive of man's spiritual nature. But if this is so, then his railing against the specific abuses in society are undercut, because there is no remedy except to give up sexual relations altogether, even for the purpose of bearing children. This is the most bizarre part of the novel. One cannot doubt that Pozdnyshev's views are Tolstoy's own, for Tolstoy wrote an afterword in which he outlined in uncompromising expository form what he was trying to say in *The Kreutzer Sonata*; what he says is essentially what Pozdnyshev has said. In *Anna Karenina* Tolstoy perceived for the first time the destructive power of physical passion. His inability to explain its place in the world he had created up to then produced that troubling ambiguity of attraction and fear that we feel in the presence of Anna's enigmatic fate. It was Tolstoy's incertitude that abetted the peculiar suspension of judgment characteristic of the novel. By the time he wrote *The Kreutzer Sonata* he had come to terms with the new force and was once again the dogmatist bent on annihilating what he could not answer.

The Kreutzer Sonata shows, if nothing else, that Tolstoy was not able to distance his disgust with sex sufficiently to turn the theme to the service of art. He is more successful in *The Devil* and *Father Sergius*, but not as successful as he will be in handling the theme of death, which is pervasive in his later works. Death had haunted him from his earliest works—one will remember the mother's death in *Childhood*—but it had not invaded his consciousness with the same power as it does in the works after *Anna Karenina*. Reality had always been unknowable for him. Indeed, the acknowledgment that reality is unknowable—the acknowledgment made by Pierre in prison—was the condition of the right kind of experiential knowing by way of an absorption of self in the immediate, but incomprehensible, flow of sensuous data before one. Death, however, brings to Tolstoy the terror and consciousness that there may not be any direction to the flow of historical reality and that sensuous immediacy may be spectral. But he refuses to give in to this fear. His faith that there is a right experience, which exists in nature and is accessible to man, remains unaltered. Imitation, art, society, intellectualism continue to distort experience, as do the subjective impulses of grief, regret, and compassion as well as the myriad attempts to bend reality to our needs.

The way to that right experience continues to be by absorption in oneself and not in things outside oneself, but the self one lives for now is a divine self. The answers to the king's three questions in this tale of 1903 are much the same that Tolstoy gave in the early tales: one attends to what is at hand at the present moment. Only the injunction to do good would be new, for in the earlier works, if one absorbed oneself in what was at hand, one would do good without effort or consciousness, as Natasha and Pierre do in their sacramental moments. The injunction to do good, with its implication of conscious effort, indicates some doubt on Tolstoy's part that goodness comes by itself. Tolstoy is being increasingly assaulted with terrors—real or imagined—that he had not faced in the works before *Anna Karenina*. Although this awareness of certain tragic aspects of life comes very much to the forefront of his works now, what is even more noticeable is the reaffirmation that life can be true and good.

Tolstoy's *Anna Karenina*: The Self's Negativity

Maire Jaanus Kurrik

The novel comes of age in the age of negativity. In order to encompass the pluralizations and multiplications produced by negativity, the novel's structure grows more complex, strained, and ironic. In [George] Eliot, irony seeks to absorb, to organize, and to point to a genetic origin and to the aim of this multiplicity. In Austen, the authorial irony becomes a submission to a Socratic unknown knowable, while the form reaches a resolution of its ironic contradictions, and stasis. The novel does not abandon the goal of totality, though the totality to be achieved has to be projected into the future. The increased pressure and complexity both of the diachronic and synchronic dimensions makes a synthesis in the present unavailable. Whereas in these two novels, as in Hegel and Goethe, the logos becomes divided between the yes and the no, being and nothingness, without being finally sundered, in Tolstoy the logos is split. This sundering has profound consequences both for the form of the novel and the development of its characters. In *Anna Karenina* there is no projection of a totality into the future, because the logos is no longer remediable dialectically in a rational or symbolic way. The unity that Levin achieves is like a dream, momentary and fleeting, in a lived reality of chronic dissociation and perplexity.

As the affirmation of a totality in the present loses its ground and validity, the novel's sense of formlessness and insubstantiality increases, and both are viewed, at first, not as conditions of art, but of consciousness. For Hegel the insubstantiality was a consequence of self-consciousness. For him the negation of substance and the body was less an intentional than a necessary oblivion, brought about by the mind's concern with its own inwardness. Thus

From *Literature and Negation*. © 1979 by Columbia University Press.

someone like Dorothea Brooke may mistake the denial for the body as a Protestant or puritanical demand, but for Eliot and Hegel it is a drive of consciousness which incorporates the body and then passes beyond it. Existent, objective bodies, even that of the self, are no longer felt to be adequate or objective correlatives for or expressions of the self's explosive inwardness. As far as content is concerned, the novel comes to be a bodiless work of art. As Hegal saw, it is not Christianity, but the development of our own consciousness that demands the denial of the body. But the price of this denial is that strange sense of insubstantiality, perplexity, and groundlessness that comes to haunt consciousness everywhere in the novel.

By contrast, in Tolstoy, consciousness in its spiritual striving appears to remain grounded in its body, in its bodily-affective unity, in its own objectivity, its knowledge of itself as an object. This perhaps above all gives Tolstoy's novels their singular Homeric quality, their sense of being epical. As in the Homeric epic, everything in Tolstoy is externalized, presented in its bodily objectivity and externality. Everything becomes fully visible and palpable, acquiring a body in space and time. For Tolstoy, as for his artist, Mikhaylov, the things in the world are already there: they have only to be perceived, recorded, and revealed. Mikhaylov speaks of creation as a process of "removing the wrappings," where one must take care not to spoil the thing that is already there as an existent.

If Levin saves himself from nihilism, it is primarily because he can experience himself both as a consciousness and a body, as subject and object. Momentarily grounded in himself as an object, he can escape the anxiety that is time and consciousness, and experience stillness. Such a moment of stillness occurs to him when he is mowing. The body absorbs consciousness, giving him "moments of oblivion" and "unconscious intervals"—ultimately also of the body itself—so that "his arms no longer seemed to swing the scythe, but the scythe itself his whole body, so conscious and full of life; and as if by magic, regularly and definitely without a thought being given to it, the work accomplished itself of its own accord." The miracle of the body in its own pure reality is that it puts us in contact with other objects, energizing them and giving them an existence and power of their own, as happens here between Levin and the scythe.

A different kind of moment of unconsciousness occurs to Levin the morning when he is waiting to make his official proposal to Kitty. On this morning it is, in fact, a deep sense of detachment from all the conditions of material existence including dependence on his own body that brings him to gaze unthinkingly on the world. On that morning his body is there and not there. It is effortlessly there as an unreal power. "He was sure that he could fly upwards or knock down the corner of a house, were it necessary." It is in the body and not in his consciousness alone that his heightened state of existence is registered. When one lives unconsciously, it is the body that lives, and it is that unconscious, nonthinking bodily affirmation of life that makes us receptive to the objective. To be deeply immersed in the self is to come upon the reality or unreality of the body, its independent existence and support, and the gift of this bodily life is a perception of the objective world in its autonomy, completeness, and singularity. Tolstoy then writes what is no doublt one of the most beautiful passages of the book:

> And what he then saw he never saw again. Two children going to school, some pigeons that flew down from the roof, and a few loaves put outside a baker's window by an invisible hand touched him particularly. These loaves, the pigeons, and the two boys seemed creatures not of this earth. It all happened at the same time; one of the boys ran after a pigeon and looked smilingly up at Levin; the pigeon flapped its wings and fluttered up, glittering in the sunshine amid the snow-dust that trembled in the air; from the window came the scent of fresh-baked bread and the loaves were put out. All these things were so unusually beautiful that Levin laughed and cried with joy.

For a moment, Levin catches the perfect particularity of everything in the world. He sees the objects in their perfect objectivity. Everything is separate, individual, and autonomous, but complete and perfect in itself— the two boys, the pigeons, the loaves. Perfect bodily subjectivity makes him capable of perfect objectivity. It allows him to perceive and receive the objects in the world with perfect perceptual clarity. But even in the midst of this experience of bodily reality, with Levin immersed in himself to the point of oblivion because what is about to be fulfilled has to do with his deepest fantasies, Tolstoy writes: "And what he then saw he never saw again." This moment in which he sees the perfection of the most ordinary things in life is a unique singular moment, the gift of his stillness and suspendedness in an imminent satisfaction, the gift of his anxietylessness. The moment is swept away in temporality, unrecoverable: "never" reminds us that all these perfect particulars are awash in temporality and that temporality is the true god of this novel.

Levin's experience with objectivity is almost a model of how all relations involuntarily occur and can be (a mutual letting be), but in the human sphere all relationships are those of anxiety, as they also are for Levin, with Kitty and his son. But Levin—even when he fails in his search for right relationships with which to comprehend his world either ethically, rationally, logically, or psychologically — can and always does maintain his relationship to himself as a body. The bodily-affective is the ground equally of his "senseless joy" and his "senseless grief," a ground of affirmation that enables him to withstand the meaninglessness and nihilism that he so clearly perceives with his consciousness. Levin's religious feelings are not an illusion for him because they are grounded, not in God, but in the unthinking life of himself as a body. Levin's body is for him the ground of a complex set of relations, of himself to his metaphysical moments, to his work, to others, and to his duty to others.

From the beginning Levin recognizes and acknowledges his need for another who will recognize him and his desires, another who will say, "All that interests him interests me." Levin is the "stranger" in the world of this novel, its greatest individualist, and yet he is the one who does not recognize his core as individual and singular. He experiences his need for Kitty and her presence in conjunction with his own existence. He is the paradox of the alienated and solitary man who yet feels that he is, at his core, two. He acts like the autonomous, singular, ontic individual, like the old "one," but he feels that he is coexistence. For him the old riddle of man has become not a riddle of the one but of two. Furthermore, his new riddle is mysterious because the sense of coexistence cannot be defined by reason. It can only be felt.

Levin believes what his nihilistic era teaches, that reason is nihil, nothing. It is nihil because it yields no meaning or purpose. It can establish neither God nor an ethic. Reason is no longer meaning-giving as it had been in Hegel. Reason only sees death and individual egos in a struggle for self-preservation. This perception drives Levin to despair and to the idea of suicide. He feels that his voided reason gnaws at him, making it impossible for him to live without knowing why he does. In his *Confession*, Tolstoy acknowledges having felt the same dilemma: "No matter how often I may be told, 'You cannot understand the meaning of life, so do not think about it, but live,' I can no longer do it: I have already done it too long. I cannot now help seeing day and night going round and bringing me to death. That is all I see, for that alone is true. All else is false." For both Tolstoy and Levin, reason has grown purely negative, but the need for reason, for a meaning persists.

Levin feels that the definition of the ego that the nihilists give is not the truth: mere self-preservation and self-love is not enough and not a reason for living and persisting. Levin knows that his love for others is undemonstrable but true. "But the law of loving others could not be discovered by reason, because it is unreasonable." Levin reaffirms "the meaning of goodness" and God after, and because he discovers that his soul is two and not one. This "objectivity" in the self prompts him to affirm his ethical relatedness to others and their coexistence with himself. And this relatedness to others feels like a meaning.

Levin curbs the demands of his questing and questioning reason by making them bend to the unreasonable and irrational law of loving others, of being in relationships of concrete love and obligation. He feels that his innate need for love and the benefits of love are tied to an ethics, an innate knowledge of good and evil that has been given to him. Yet we know that it was only by chance and accident, and thanks to Levin's own deep harmony with his bodily-affective life, that his negation of Kitty was overcome and that the pain of his rejected love was turned into the good of relatedness, which feels like a meaning. Furthermore, we know that what he calls his "innate" knowledge of good and evil is but the content of his inherited and traditional superego.

Levin feels that he must trust that his subjective need for meaning is a testament to something and not to nothing. Not reason, but intuitions, actions, and feelings overcome nihilism and are a constant demonstration of purposiveness. Levin is intuitively and "irrationally" willing to believe that the world picture is, ethically, rationally, and theologically as his forefathers had believed it to be. He accepts as valid the traditional-conventional world picture, knowing that it cannot be submitted to rational scrutiny. He reaffirms Hegel's vision of a purposive force and becoming without the aid of reason. He discovers that his "unconscious" or his inherited self and superego are positive and affirmative, and that his conscious mind is negative and nihilistic. He also knows that this gap between his consciousness and his unconscious can never be healed. A dissonance—the constant potential of a disjunction—will always remain part of his experience. He will again and again experience the negativity of his mind and have moments when his reason will question and torment the validity of what he believes. The Hegelian possibility of affirming the world and the self by reason is over for him, yet he holds on to the telos that is at the heart of the world, because subjectively he cannot do without a purpose or accept an irrational world picture such as that, for example, of Schopenhauer. What Levin comes to believe—that meaninglessness is a product of consciousness whereas the unconscious is meaningful, purposive, life-affirming, and antisuicidal—comes to be demonstrated in Anna, who in her final lucid moments submits to the evidence of her consciousness.

Levin's irrational self affirms that what Lukacs called "totality" still exists. Levin projects the old metaphor with only a part of himself, metonymically. Hence he will forever reexperience the opposition and contradiction between his consciousness and unconsciousness, the fact that they were not designed for each other and not designed with the end of intrasubjective harmony in mind. Levin affirms God because he cannot stay in or endure the suspended state of irony and paradox of the Lukácsian novelist. He needs to draw the old gods of the epic, as it were, into his present reality. For him, "the present, non-existent God" has to become present. The old customs function for him as the epic functioned for Lukács. It is in the old customs that "totality" lives. Like the Lukácsian novelist, Levin seeks God in the old forms into which He has retreated, but unlike the Lukácsian novelist, Levin also makes the leap of faith. He cannot live in a world abandoned by God, giving his complete assent to incompleteness and negativity. Yet, Levin also knows that even after having found God, he may lose Him again and again. His relationship to God is somewhat analogous to his relationship to Kitty, a relationship both of marriage and "divorce." For although Levin longs for God as he had longed for union with Kitty, his sense of disjunction from both is also always potentially present, his sense that he is alienated from her, that she is, at moments, a "stranger" for him.

For Levin the other is duty and work. He feels his coexistence ethically. Anna feels it primarily passionately, and comes to destroy the other whom she needs. Anna also knows that the self is two, but she "unethically" perverts love into mutual suffering. She affirms the need for coexistence in despair. In the world of this novel as a whole, the coexistence is silently felt, but not spoken about. And this sense of felt coexistence is also feared because it is coterminous with another perception that all the characters have, that the other who is needed is also a stranger. Thus Stiva feels like a "stranger" to Dolly, as Vronsky does to Anna, and even Kitty at moments to Levin. Each one suffers terribly when experiencing this strangeness of the other to the self or of the self to the other, but no one can fully overcome the experience. All come to see at times that the image of the other lies silently in their soul, but they do not and cannot speak to this other.

Individualism is criticized and negated in the novel, and yet it is the singular, autonomous, and monological individual who dominates this novel. Each one feels that he has to achieve and determine himself alone and in isolation, and yet all know that they are not alone and cannot determine themselves alone. The paradox of isolate being in a world of coexistence is one with which each character has to contend. Thereby the very problems and contradictions of isolate existence versus coexistence, and the ethics of each, achieve a far clearer delineation in Tolstoy than in Eliot. What determines the quality of each character's life is how each handles this dialectic of strangeness and coexistence. Anna insists on the lovelessness, strangeness, and isolation only to demonstrate that she and Vronsky are one. She destroys their lives to reveal the alienation in love, its pain and reality, and its untruth.

Anna also lives in the body, the bodily-affective, as does Levin and everything in the world of Tolstoy, but she lives in a very conscious and ethical relation to the body, coming increasingly to experience its potential for dread. The body becomes not an "opening" for her—as it does for Levin in birth, death, and marriage—into a sense of relatedness, but a source of disrelatedness, of lovelessness, solitude, and the ugly, meaningless particularity of things. That her disruption and distress begins in the body becomes particularly evident in chapter 11 of part 2, where her first sexual union with Vronsky is described in terms of a complicity in the murder of a body, a complicity which fills Anna with disgust and horror. Anna feels that her body has been murdered, deprived of live. This feeling is a sign of her ethical complexity as well as of the fact that she fears genital sexuality and finds it difficult to accept. What is tragic for her is that her need for assurance that she is loved will always have to be sought in sexuality. Hereafter, she always deals in her dialectical relationship to herself with one part that is absent, condemned, and dead. Her ambivalent sense of her body becomes most obvious when she finally chooses to die, not, for example, by taking morphium, but by being mutilated and destroyed by a murderous and punishing object like the train. The train punishes her declassed, mysterious, peasant-like body.

When Anna "destroys" her body, she destroys and warps her unconscious, for in Tolstoy unconsciousness, or as much of it as he knows, is almost synonymous with the body. The death of her body weighs on her from the beginning as a concrete, disorienting nothingness, a weight which no longer allows her to think clearly, even though she struggles with increasing obsession to maintain this body and its beauty artificially. When Vronsky grows irritated and weary of her domination of him by her beauty and calls her "unnatural," he wounds her deeply precisely because he confirms what she long knew and felt. It is in their first sexual encounter that Anna loses her ordinary self-feeling and abandons her libidinal investment in the most vital part of herself, her body. If Anna ultimately feels left alone in a world devoid of love, it is precisely because her intense unconscious guilt long ago produced in her a feeling of emptiness, a sense that she had destroyed part of her interiority by her badness. The relationship to the other depends on the internal subjective relationship to self grounded in the body, a relationship which is disrupted in Anna at the beginning.

The "human self," as Kierkegaard argued, is a synthesis of the soulish-bodily, grounded in Spirit. It is the unity of the body with the soul (with will, intellect, and imagination). A disorder in the spiritual relationship will reveal itself in bodily and affective traces or, conversely, certain disorders in the latter are signs of the spiritual disrelationship. For Kierkegaard, there is dread in all erotic experience, and especially in childbirth because the suspension of spirit is felt as dread, and the erotic is the discovery of sensuousness that does temporarily break the self-relationship of the self to itself. Anna comes to experience the break permanently as guilt and shame. She immediately feels disconnected both from her pleasure and from spirit, and struggles initially to recover from her spiritual alienation by guilt and shame. In a sense her spirit, as Kierkegaard describes it, looks back over its shoulder at itself in the body, which is not its proper abode, with dread. By her act, Anna confines herself to the perpetual reexperiencing of erotic dread. She must seek being—self-perpetuation and relationship—in the erotic nothing that she dreads; when she is no longer capable of seeking being in what has truly become a stale and empty experience of nothingness, she turns and comes to seek nothingness itself in a loss of faith in being. Thus Anna comes fully to experience what Kierkegaard called the "prodigious contradiction (*Wiederspruch*) that the immortal spirit is characterized as sex." In Kierkegaard the sundering from spirit, its exclusion in the erotic, is felt more completely and spiritually in women precisely because they are more sensuous. Kierkegaard and Tolstoy recognize the body as the ground of the instincts, but they relate the instincts themselves, in different ways, to consciousness rather than the unconscious.

As soon as Anna meets Vronsky she feels both "frightened" and "happy." She feels the apprehension, alarm, adventure that Kierkegaard calls the approach of possibility, the sense of a new, more complete and more animated synthesis of the human self. But this apprehension of becoming is always a feeling simultaneously of nothingness and something, of dread and being. Anna feels dread because on the one hand love is a risk, a recklessness, the possibility of loss, emptiness, and dependence; on the other hand, it is a possibility of fulfillment and union. But in the erotic union, the synthesis and linkage is always temporary, fragile, breaking. Furthermore, from the beginning Anna's own spiritual conscience rejects the linkage as a guilty one. She projects her guilt and, accompanying it, her need for punishment onto Vronsky as his desire to leave and abandon her. This is the source of her demon, her spurts of malevolence toward Vronsky. She blames herself for her desire and also blames him for arousing it. Her punishing dreams and perceptions of doubleness are her own divided perceptions of herself in ethical and erotic terms which she cannot make cohere. Her dissociation is the manifestation of her intrapsychic conflict and a primitive defense against it.

She experiences what Hegel calls "the essential moment, viz. that of breaking up into extremes with opposite characteristics" as a permanent moment that she cannot overcome. She lives more and more in the relentless atmosphere of the self's negativity.

In her illness and close brush with death, she reasserts her ethical sense; as soon as she is well, she sees only how much Karenin's ears stick out. Her inalienable consciousness of the body dominates again. She feels that her wholeness depends on Vronsky's attraction to her, and thus all her possessive impulses are set in play: to keep him, attract him, test him, repossess him — and always by way of her physical beauty. The conflict narrows down to a mutual conflict of wills, of self-preservation, in which every departure of Vronsky becomes an occasion for a traumatic scene. Anna's urge to own and control turns into an urge to punish what she cannot control. Her suicide is an active mutual punishment, of him for his abandonment of her, of herself for her guilt, and also a way of putting an end to the terror, the suspense of being or not being loved. The suicide is a part of their mutual struggle for recognition, their mistrust, lack of communication, their fear of a crisis and their desire also to provoke a crisis in order to end the dilemma. Suicide has a terrible ambiguity here and the characteristics of a synthesis, a total solution to all the problems. Finally her inner, desperate sense of self-guilt, hatred, ugliness, and lovelessness become the characteristics of the objective world as a whole.

> "Is any kind — not of happiness even but of freedom from torture — possible? No! No! . . . It is impossible! Life is sundering us, and I am the cause of his unhappiness and he of mine, and neither he nor I can be made different. Every effort has been made, but the screws do not act . . . A beggar woman with a baby. She thinks I pity her. Are we not all flung into the world only to hate each other, and therefore to torment ourselves and others? There go schoolboys — they are laughing. Serezha?" she remembered. "I thought I loved him, too, and was touched at my own tenderness for him. Yet I live without him and exchanged his love for another's, and did not complain of the change as long as the other love satisfied me." And she thought with disgust of what she called "the other love."

Anna's relation to her erotic experience remains radically conscious, spiritual, and ethical. She cannot tolerate the idea of lovelessness that she anticipates in Vronsky and sees in herself in her relationship to her son. The fundamental fact of fickleness, infidelity, and disrelationship is at the core of her negative spiritual vision. "It's all untrue, all lies, all deception, all evil!" Anna caps the truth of her body by reason. "Reason has been given to man to enable him to escape from his troubles," she hears a lady saying, and Anna "reasons": "Why not put out the candle, if there is nothing more to look at?"

If we look back from Anna's and Levin's experience of their reason and their body to the scheme we derived [elsewhere] from Ficino, we can see that we have come almost full circle. Reason apprehends not God but the nihil. Anna gives her assent to this apprehension, Levin does not. The body, however, which had been in Ficino a source of torment, contradiction, and unreason, is now the very ground for the apprehension of God. When the split logos *is* healable, albeit only momentarily, it is so only in a self grounded in the body, in a self that assents to the body and its unreason, its unreasonable law of two, of union and birth. For Anna, who has in a sense lost and "murdered" her body, this indispensable ground for the spiritual synthesis, the synthesis is no longer available.

What is so compelling in Tolstoy's novel is the equal spiritual strength of Levin's affirmation and Anna's negation. Both emerge from a deep and solitary need to create a synthesis in the self and for the self. Both emerge from a spiritual persistence to relate the self to a totality and to have a clear answer of yes or no to the experience of existence, a persistence which echoes the old hankering after a clear vision of being or nothingness, a hankering after the knowledge of the ground of existence. What is so frightening and powerful as well is exactly the fact that the answer of yes or no appears ultimately, as in Kierkegaard, like a choice in the self, rather than as an answer forced on us by objective conditions. The objective conditions, though very present and powerful, are ultimately not what tips the scale one way or the other. The self itself finally makes the choice: it can readily and easily be either a yes or a no. It is the very identities between Anna and Levin that make the difference in the ultimate choices so troubling and mysterious. By a miracle, Levin leaps out of spiritual dread into being, ethical existence, goodness, and a faith in relatedness. By an equal dread of spirit Anna leaps to nothingness, meaninglessness, disbelief. These are disjunct possibilities in fundamentally the same world and the same self.

It is this very disjunction of the stories of Anna and Levin which early critics immediately criticized as a "basic deficiency in construction," as "a lack of architectonics," and which Tolstoy answered by a series of somewhat vague rebuttals. He claimed that the architectonics was perfect because the links were precisely as indirect, as invisible as he had wished them to be. He claimed that the unity of the structure was an "inner continuity" based not on an idea but "on something else" which could not possibly be expressed directly in words. Yet Tolstoy also said that everything he wrote was guided by the need to bring together ideas linked among themselves," which, however, became debased and meaningless when directly expressed. A close formal study of the novel, of course, reveals that not only Levin's and Anna's but everyone's experience in the novel is a repetition with variations.

This formal repetition is both more "indirect" and "invisible" than any plot coherence could be. It points to the "inner continuity" of isolation and self-disjunction experienced by each, and hidden by each from the other almost like a shame. This negative linkage—this continuity of discontinuity—brings together "ideas linked among themselves," and brings into relief the fundamental concept of character here: the idea that character is a consciousness alone, for all its social ties, acting on itself, concerned with its own spiritual synthesis (which cannot be achieved), ignorant of other consciousnesses. The architectonics emphasizes what the representation of more direct social and plot relations might obscure, self-consciousness in its solitude and self-disjunction.

Tolstoy's architectonics allows the fundamentally monological nature of the self to appear, its ontic, epistemic, emotional, and bodily solitude, and the immense perturbation that it suffers from coexistence. One revealing authorial phrase reinforces this effect of the architectonics, namely when Tolstoy comments that someone "did not know this." What each ultimately does not know is some crucial psychic fact about themselves and about others they love. It is the fact of the lack of self-knowledge that makes them both unable to see that they are making choices and to make these choices more consciously. Thus each character faces the dilemma of what to do, and puts off approaching the dilemma actively by saying "things will right themselves," by drifting and postponing (unaware that this too is a choice); or the characters feel that the choices are ultimately imposed on them.

The other aspect of their monological being has to do with the characters' lack of knowledge of the other and their lack of a drive to know the other. They live with each other, unaware that they do not really know each other, or they brush this awareness aside, repressing it as a kind of aberrant idea when it does come, as it does to Levin before he marries Kitty—a sense of panic that he does not know her, nor she him or herself: " 'But do I know her thoughts, wishes, or feelings?' a voice suddenly whispered. . . . 'Supposing she does not love me? . . . Supposing she does not herself know what she is doing?'" But failure to face the fact that not even love gives us insight into the other makes the characters fail to pursue the dialogue that is necessary for understanding. They act on assumptions about the other based on the self's monologue with itself, or its hopes and fears. Notable in Anna is her almost chronic inability to use and confront words. She fears words and yet takes wordlessness as an important sign for feeling. She does not know that the only way we can penetrate others is by dialogue, that dialogue alone turns us into subjects in relationship to each other. But imagination, with its objectifications and projections, keeps the other an object.

Thus the character's perceptions of each other are fundamentally metonymic; they are based everywhere on a lack of full presence or being, a part substituting for the whole. It is this metonymic and projected relationship that is so clearly demonstrated in the tragic failure of communication between Anna and Vronsky. But it is also evident in lesser ways in Dolly's relationship to her children, whom she does not know when she fears at moments that they will become evil, or in Levin's final moment, when he decides to keep his vision a secret from Kitty, an act which echoes Varenka and Koznyshev's lost moment of speaking. It is this fundamental penchant of the characters to remain monologic, working things out in solitude, including their relationship to crucial and nearby others, and the metonymic, partial relationship of the characters to each other that constitute the troubling and overall effect of Tolstoy's architectonics. Tolstoy's clarity in representing this becomes the possibility of a vision that criticizes this entire manner of self-existence and coexistence—one so characteristic of the nineteenth century, so inadequate, and so obviously based on an old religious model where the relationship to the self and to the spiritual other could not be anything but private, monologic, and partial.

In a world of coexistence, a subjectivity that asks primarily "What am I?" is not enough. An ethical self constituted in solitude with itself or even with God is not yet ethically adequate. There is a level at which the hidden linkage of Tolstoy becomes a form of ironic criticism of a certain kind of subjectivity which gives the novel a nontragic dimension despite its predominantly tragic form. Tolstoy's structuration demonstrates simultaneously the practice and truth of the Kierkegaardian notion of spiritual selfhood and self-development in the nineteenth-century world and the inadequacy of this notion of selfhood in a social world of coexistence. In Kierkegaard, man is by definition spiritual and the presence of spirit in him will either help him to find God or, undeveloped, will torment him and make him seek an identity against spirit, an identity in nothing. "God tempts no man" and "is not tempted by anyone," says Kierkegaard, but "every man is tempted by himself." What Kierkegaard's spiritual self-dialectic omits is the self's relationship to the other human self. In Tolstoy's characters we find fundamentally the same omission. They come into a positive relationship to themselves and to others via the detour of God. Without the supportive and radiant transcendental moment, the self sinks into despair and disrelationships. The Tolstoyan "human self," unlike the developed "theological self" of Kierkegaard, can only maintain its synthesis temporarily. Furthermore, the "human" self needs a dialectic, which must in essence be dialogical, with another "human" self. The clearest sign of the split logos of this artistic world on the level of coexistence is the absence or inadequacy of full, human dialogue. This absence or inadequacy, which is not acceptable, contradicts the tragic form's tendency to accept everything as inevitable. Eliot sought relief from the tragic vision of her novel by the projection of a nontragic future, and sometimes, by the direct censure of the inadequacy of a particular moral will. In Tolstoy, there is neither the projection nor the censure, and yet there is an opening up of the tragic form by the critical representation. In both, despite the difference in degree, there is an ambiguity toward the tragic form that is in itself one of the most intriguing aspects of their novels.

The world is disjunct, so are the lives of the characters, and so is the self. In the self, the clearest sign of the split logos is the depths of the experience of the body-mind split. All these disjunctions are a truth of which the formal plot disjunction is but a small and necessary reflection.

In Tolstoy's novel the Hegelian conjunction of the self's negativity with Reason disintegrates. The self in its development through self-negativity has difficulty in overcoming the divisions, splits, oppositions, and antitheses that it itself produces. There is no longer any ultimate meaning-giving, rational force to help heal, synthesize, and reunite the perplexing consequences of negativity. Anna's absolute despair lives on in Levin's sense of disjunction at those moments when his reason will question his unreasonable persistence in living. Anna's life is but an absolute dramatization of what will continue to happen to Levin. In the actual, meaningless world of becoming, true despair is as little reversible into joyous synthesis as the logic of concrete bodily-affective experience is defiable. The novel leaves us finally with a double vision: a sense that on the one hand everything depends on the individual's monologue and dialectic with the synthesizing spirit, as in Kierkegaard, and on the other, that the crucial determining factors are, first dialogue, and then, respectively, Levin's positive and Anna's negative relationship to the body, the ground of human truth, spirit, and coexistence.

Tolstoy and the Forms of Life: "Inexorable Law"

Martin Price

Tolstoy's intensity is not simply the effect of brilliant gesture or image. In fact, Proust dismisses observation altogether:

> This is not the work of an observing eye but of a thinking mind. Every so-called stroke of observation is simply the clothing, the proof, the instance, of a law, a law of reason or of unreason, which the novelist has laid bare. And our impression of the breadth and life is due precisely to the fact that none of this is the fruit of observation, but that every deed, every action, being no other than any expression of law, one feels oneself moving amid a throng of laws—why, since the truth of these laws is established for Tolstoi by the inward authority they have exercised over his thinking, there are some which we are still baffled by.
>
> (*Marcel Proust on Art and Literature 1896-1916*, trans. S. T. Warner)

One can see what Proust means in those mordant ironies through which Tolstoy looks beyond his characters' vision and instantiates laws in epigram. We see Anna "calling to mind Karenin with every detail of his figure, his way of speaking, and his character, and making him responsible for everything bad she could find in him, forgiving him nothing because of the terrible thing she had done to him" (bk. 2, chap. 23). Much later, there is a terrible parallel when she has had her last quarrel with Vronsky: "All the cruelest things a coarse man could say she imagined him to have said to her, and she did not forgive him for them just as if he had really said them" (bk. 7, chap. 26).

Or we have Anna telling Vronsky of her pregnancy. He has been troubled

From *Forms of Life: Character and Moral Imagination in the Novel.* © 1983 by Yale University. Yale University Press, 1983.

by all the subterfuges both of them, not without shame, have had to practice; and he has begun to feel "revulsion against something: against Karenin,
against himself, against the whole world—he was not sure which." Anna's
son Seryozha, in his own uncertainties, has made Vronsky feel ill at ease
and aroused in him once more "that strange feeling of blind revulsion which
he had experienced of late." And with Anna's news, Vronsky turns pale and
lowers his head—Anna thinks with gratitude that he understands the full
significance of the event. "But," Tolstoy proceeds, "she was wrong in thinking
that he understood the significance . . . as she, a woman, understood it. At
this news he felt the onrush of that strange feeling of revulsion for someone;
but at the same time he realized that the crisis he had wished for had now
come" (bk. 2, chap. 22). One must suspect that some of Vronsky's revulsion
is for Anna and for the power she has over him; that is a possibility she
cannot allow herself to entertain until later. Again, at the steeplechase before
Vronsky's fall, Anna is outraged by Karenin's protracted conversation with
an important colleague. "All he cares about is lies and keeping up appearances,"
she thinks, without considering "what exactly she wanted of her husband
or what she would have liked him to be. Nor did she realize that Karenin's
peculiar loquaciousness that day . . . was merely an expression of his inner
anxiety and uneasiness" (bk. 2, chap. 28). In each of these cases there is a
false estimation or an irrational judgment; Anna is too guilty or eager or
bitter to see what the author discloses. In each case there is cause enough
for Anna's misapprehension, but Tolstoy's immediate ironic rectification has
the effect of invoking what Proust calls his laws of reason and unreason.

As soon as characters seem to obey laws of which they are unaware,
the implications become ambiguous. Are they too much obsessed to see what
is really there? Or are they too deeply committed to make a cool canvass
of fact? Is Anna's obliviousness a form of self-absorption and fantasy, or is
it the integrity of a woman who "must live her feelings right through"?
Against her intensity we can set those compromises and dissonances that mark
most lives. The novel opens with the dissolution of a family structure. It
is a temporary dissolution, but the restoration will never be complete. Stiva
Oblonsky awakens at eight o'clock as always; but as he stretches out his
feet for his slippers and his hand for his dressing gown, he realizes that he
has slept on the sofa: for his wife Dolly has learned of his affair with the
former governess; and when she expressed her horror, Oblonsky's face quite
involuntarily "smiled its usual kind and, for that reason, rather foolish smile."
It is the smile that Stiva regrets rather than the adultery, for the smile had
the force of a blow for his wife. She responded with bitter words and has
refused to see him.

Stiva is pained at his wife's grief. He has persuaded himself that she has pretended not to know of his infidelities, and in fact that is the attitude Dolly will assume thereafter, "letting herself be deceived, despising him, and most of all herself, for that weakness." On the occasion of this first discovery, she is divided between the need to take strong action and the pull of habit and convention. She feels outrage at the sight of his pity because it is so visibly less than love; but she is more troubled by the fear of estrangement. Stiva recognizes the "usual answer life gives to the most complicated and insoluble questions": to live from day to day and to lose oneself in the "dream of life" (bk. 1, chap. 2).

While the Oblonskys' marriage is not a very happy one and will never get better, it is, at any rate, a structure of habits and responsibilities which, however imperfectly realized, is still a refuge from the intolerable. But it *is* imperfectly realized. We see this in Stiva's treatment of his children. When his daughter embraces him, he holds her and strokes her neck as he asks after her mother. Stiva knows that he does not care so much for his son, and he always tries therefore to treat both children in the same way. But his son senses the effort and responds to it rather than its pretense. When Stiva asks if her mother is cheerful, his daughter knows that there has been a quarrel and that her father is fully aware of her mother's disturbance but pretends that he is not. She blushes for him. He perceives that and blushes in turn.

We see the persistence of Stiva's neglect when Dolly takes the children to their country cottage in order to save expenses. Stiva has gone to Petersburg to further his career, and he has taken almost all the money in the house. He was asked by Dolly to have the cottage put in comfortable shape. He looked to the externals but neglected essential repairs. Nor was this the lack of the will to be a "solicitous father and husband." He has meant well, or at least has meant to mean well; but the roof still leaks, the cattle have been loose in the garden, there are no pots and pans, there are not enough milk and butter and eggs. The bailiff whom Stiva chose for "his handsome and respectful appearance" is of no help at all. Dolly is in despair until her old servant Matryona sets everything right, and gradually Dolly recovers her spirits and recaptures her great pride in her children (bk. 3, chap. 7).

On a fine spring day after much preparation of their clothes, Dolly takes her children to communion. The occasion requires that Dolly dress beautifully so as "not to spoil the general effect" and she is pleased with the admiration that she and her six children elicit from the peasants in church. And the children behave beautifully. The smallest, Lily, takes the sacrament and delightfully repeats, in English, Oliver Twist's words, "I want some more, please." It is a day of all but unclouded joy. Dolly feels both love and confidence. Near the river where they have all gone bathing, she falls into conversation with the peasant women. Dolly finds it hard to leave these women, "so absolutely identical were their interests." All the world about her seems for once to belong to Dolly, to reflect her own feelings and to embrace her with affection and admiration (bk. 3, chap. 8).

The rapture cannot be sustained. As they return to the cottage, Levin is waiting. He has come at Stiva's urging, but he does not want Dolly to feel that Stiva has foisted responsibility on him. Dolly not only perceives that, but she is touched by the "fine perception and delicacy" with which Levin tries to spare her the shame of her husband's neglect. Here as with the exchange of blushes between Stiva and his daughter, there is a second-order response, a response to a response. Tolstoy uses it characteristically to emphasize the implicit meanings that are shared within a form of life, but perhaps become more oblique and difficult as the form is compromised (bk. 3, chap. 9).

Dolly wants Levin to know that Kitty is coming to visit her. She has suspected that he proposed and was rejected, and now, as she senses his anger, she tries to meet it with an account of Kitty's suffering. The more precisely Levin recalls that rejection, the more uncharitable he becomes and the more determined not to see Kitty. Dolly tells him he is absurd, but she says it with tenderness. She creates a distraction by addressing her daughter in French and requiring that Tanya answer in French. This, as now everything about the family, strikes Levin as disagreeable. "Teach French and unteach sincerity," he thinks to himself, not imagining that Dolly considered that danger for a long while before deciding it was worth the cost of some sincerity for her children to learn French. Levin, disenchanted, prepares to leave. The disenchantment spreads like a cloud. The children have begun to fight, and for Dolly a "great shadow seems to have fallen over her life." She "realized that these children of hers . . . were not only quite ordinary, but even bad, ill-bred children, with coarse, brutal propensities, wicked children in fact." She voices all her sorrow to Levin, and he reassures her that all children fight. But he is no longer sincere. He thinks as he leaves, "No, I won't try to show off and talk French with my children" (bk. 3, chap. 10).

Both Dolly and Levin have feelings that are spontaneous, deep, and pervasive. Their world must, in Wittgenstein's phrase, "wax or wane as a whole. As if by accession or loss of meaning." Wittgenstein's point is that our will cannot alter the facts of the world, only its limits or boundaries; it can affect our world only by making it wholly different. Tolstoy gives some of his characters an intensity of feeling that wholly alters their world. The process is faintly ludicrous even as it is touching, as in this case.

These instances may be seen as acute observation of motive and manners, as the necessary consequences of laws Tolstoy traces and confirms, as the meeting point of thematic concerns and their convergence in events of depth and resonance. Proust chooses to stress the second, to see particulars as "simply the clothing, the proof, the instance, of a law." This is in part a tribute to the sense of necessity Tolstoy gives his world; his "apparently inexhaustible fund of creation," as Proust calls it, does not need to spend itself in merely clever observations. The necessity which Proust ascribes to laws in Tolstoy he accounts for in other ways that are no less apt in his discussion of George Eliot:

> Another striking thing is the sense of gravity attached to an evil intention or to a failure of resolution, which because of the interdependence of mankind spreads its fatal repercussions in every direction; and another, the sense of the mysterious greatness of human life and the life of nature, the solemn mysteries in which we play a part while knowing no more about them than does the growing flower.
>
> (*Marcel Proust on Art and Literature, 1896–1916*)

This concatenation of lives in fatal repercussions resembles what George Eliot calls "undeviating law," "invariability of sequence," or the "inexorable law of consequences" — patterns of order which we can recognize and to which we must submit.

The capacity for submission, for what George Eliot calls "patient watching of external fact" and "silencing of preconceived notions," is a readiness to allow possibilities their emergence, a reluctance to delimit experience to what is governable and explicable. This may be a withdrawal from visible but not from conceivable relevance, and it risks the acceptance of details, events, "observations" which may threaten as well as exemplify laws. George Eliot found the "highest form" in the "highest organism, that is to say, the most varied group of relations bound together in a wholeness which again has the most varied relations with all other phenomena." We tend, today, to want to demystify a term like *organism*, which by definition represents an incalculable unity. We may recognize that the novelist often uses a few bold inconsistencies which are suggestive enough to demand of him and of us a new and more arduous effort to explain and unify. Tolstoy's boldness is so nicely judged that we are persuaded of the implicit lawfulness and consequently look for it in greater depth. I want to consider two instances.

Kitty Shcherbatsky, like Levin and Anna and even more than her sister

Dolly, cannot live a half-life or dismiss her grief over Vronsky's betrayal. We see her falling into illness that has no physical cause. She is examined by a specialist whose self-importance may be measured by his indifference to his patient's embarrassment. Kitty's mother, the Princess Shcherbatsky, feels guilty about Vronsky, and she means to be abject before the doctors. They in turn consult with each other to decide which treatment of Kitty will best satisfy her imperious mother. Dolly, who is present, asks their mother if Kitty's shame and grief are due in part to her regret that she has refused Levin, but the old princess is appalled at the thought that she is to blame for having encouraged Vronsky, and she grows angry with Dolly. Nor is she alone in her response. Kitty throws off her sister Dolly's pity with anger and cruelty: "I've enough pride," she cries, "never to let myself love a man who does not love me." And when Dolly ignores the thrust and talks directly about Levin, Kitty is all the more furious: "I shall never, *never* do what you're doing—go back to a man who has been unfaithful to you, who falls in love with another woman." Dolly is crushed by her sister's cruelty, and Kitty at last breaks down in tears. Each understands the other's feelings, and Kitty knows that she has been forgiven.

She can speak then of her changed world, so much like the one Anna will create as the climate of suicide: "everything has become odious, disgusting, and coarse to me, myself most of all. You can't imagine what disgusting thoughts I have about everything" (bk. 2, chap. 3). Later, at the German watering place Kitty tries to achieve entire selflessness and idealism, only coming at last to realize that she has misjudged and injured others in order to sustain her aspiration. She finally dismisses her role of ministering angel as a sham. "Let me be bad, but at least not a liar, not a humbug," she cries, and she realizes that she has been "deceiving herself in imagining that she could be what she wished to be." She returns to Russia cured, "calm and serene." Kitty's pride leads to difficulties both before her marriage and after; but it is a principle of vitality. Her independence and resistance to Levin's will is a far greater thing than Dolly's bitter resignation.

Vronsky is a character who shows so much growth in the early parts of the novel that we are not quite prepared, in spite of sufficient warning, for his limitations in what follows. We first see him as an immature libertine, a brilliant and wealthy officer charmed by the innocence and adoration of a young girl of high society (all of his love affairs have been outside it). "He could not possibly believe that what gave such genuine pleasure to him, and above all to her, could be wrong." But he has no affection for the conventions of family life, and the role of husband seems "alien, hostile, and above all, ridiculous." His initial shallowness is to be seen in his "pleasant feeling of purity and freshness" at the Shcherbatskys', "partly due to the fact that he had not smoked all evening, and with it a new feeling of tenderness at her love for him" (bk. 1, chap. 16). Even when Vronsky has become a great deal more serious, his sense of well-being finds its immediate expression in a consciousness of his body. "It gave him pleasure to feel the slight pain in his strong leg, it was pleasant to feel the muscular sensation of movement in his chest as he breathed." And Tolstoy enforces an incongruity: "the same bright and cold August day which made Anna feel so hopeless seemed exhilarating and invigorating to him and refreshed his face and neck, which were still glowing after the drenching he had given them under the tap." Somehow the face and neck seem awkwardly specific and trivial, just as the pride he feels after his first meeting with Anna seems touching but naive: "He looked at people as if they were things. A nervous young man . . . sitting opposite began to detest him for that look."

Vronsky's love for Anna makes him a far more serious and courageous man. He tends, it is true, to return easily to his old world of habit, and the first part of the novel ends on a somewhat ominous note, as habit recaptures the Vronsky we have so far seen in Moscow or on the train: "As always when in Petersburg, he left the house not to return till late at night." Unlike Anna, he has a role both in his regiment and in the society he frequents that gives him a secure sense of rightness; the role of a man pursuing a married woman had "something grand and beautiful about it and could never be ridiculous." He has not yet had to leave the world he has known in order to enter this new world that their love creates. The first real test of Vronsky is the steeplechase. He has, as we have seen, been troubled by the deceptions he has had to practice and has felt a sudden revulsion at the news of Anna's pregnancy. In the race a moment of doubt disables his customary, assured command of his horse, and through a terrible error he breaks the back of Frou-Frou, the nervous mare he is riding. Worst of all perhaps is the rage to which his remorse and frustration lead: he kicks the dying horse in the belly before he realizes fully what he has done. Much later, when Anna rejects his warning and insists upon going to the opera, where she will surely be snubbed, Vronsky is left behind in outrage. "And why does she put me in such a position?" he exclaims, and he upsets the table that holds soda and brandy. He tries to steady the table but only overturns it, and finally, in his vexation, he kicks it over.

Between these two events Vronsky has attempted suicide. As a man who has always needed a clear code of rules, who had an essential role in the regiment that is his only family, he finds himself suddenly humbled by Karenin's forgiveness. The forgiveness leaves Vronsky feeling "ashamed, humiliated, guilty . . . kicked out of the normal way of life. . . . Everything that had seemed so firmly established, all the rules and habits of his life, suddenly turned out to be false and inapplicable." Vronsky finds himself, as it were, outside the forms of life, without purchase or balance, awed and disgraced by the generosity and dignity of Karenin. "They had suddenly exchanged roles. Vronsky felt Karenin's greatness and his own humiliation." He has lost the grandeur of the lover, and he has lost Anna; and in that moment the love that had begun to wane altogether revives. His attempt to kill himself fails, and he has prepared instead to undertake a "flattering and dangerous mission to Tashkent" when Anna recovers and returns to him. He must resign not only the new post but his commission as well; he sets about shaping new forms of life with Anna. The new forms remain unreal; they have no rooted existence, they make no earnest demand, they carry no necessity.

ENDINGS

One way to speak of the contrast between the story of Levin and that of Anna is the expansion of Levin's life to include more and the painful contraction of Anna's life as she is excluded from those forms which have formerly sustained her. She and Vronsky have made in Italy one halfhearted attempt to create new forms, and in the sixth part of the novel that attempt is renewed in more plausible but more radically flawed forms. The sixth part of *Anna Karenina* is the most elegant in design. We move between two estates with Dolly, from Levin's to Vronsky's; and the final section brings both landlords to the provincial elections. There is, moreover, the ludicrous dandy Veslovsky, who appears at both estates. Dolly and her children are staying with Levin and Kitty. Her own country house is now, through Oblonsky's neglect, "completely dilapidated"; and Oblonsky is happy to send his family off to he country, where he can pay them occasional short visits.

With Kitty and Dolly is their mother, the princess, and the three women make raspberry jam together. Kitty feels a new relationship with her mother, something closer to equality, as they talk—three married women—about the likelihood of Varenka's receiving a proposal from Levin's brother, Koznyshev. Dolly thinks back to Stiva's courtship. Kitty asks her mother how her own marriage was settled, in what gestures or words agreement was reached. "And," Tolstoy goes on, "the three women thought about one and the same thing." It is one of those moments that Tolstoy manages with distinctive power. There is not the dissolution of membranes between people so that they become, as in Virginia Woolf, for a moment one stream of feeling. In Tolstoy, people, often locked in their own memories, participate in a common form of life.

So with a possible marriage. Koznyshev remarked with regret at Levin's wedding that he was "past all that." Varenka is a mature and selfless woman who might comfort that rather complacent intellectual. To his younger brother Levin, Koznyshev seems to lead only a spiritual existence. He is "too pure and high-minded a man" to come to terms with reality. And Kitty in turn insists that Varenka is "all spirit." There isn't, she says, "so much of this reality in her as there is in me." But the proposal fails because neither person quite wants it, and all the trivia that somehow rush to Varenka's lips have behind them her resistance to the exposure and risk of a new relationship. Koznyshev has pressed beyond his comfortable rationalization—his fidelity to the long-dead Marie. He is at the point of proposing but ready to withdraw, all too easily thrown off. And so they go on talking about mushrooms. The ludicrous, Chekhovian banalities become their defenses. "And the moment those words were uttered, both he and she understood that it was all over, that what should have been said would never be said, and their agitation, having reached its climax, began to subside."

Each of them represents a kind of half life in the novel. Varenka's conventionality and denial of life once seemed to Kitty saintliness. Koznyshev's intellectuality and condescension have had the power to shake Levin's confidence. But, in fact, each of these characters helps to define the vitality of the central figures, who risk everything because they cannot endure something less than life. Later, as the children have their tea, everyone avoids talking of what might have happened. Koznyshev and Varenka feel "like children who have failed their examinations and have to stay behind in the same class or who have been expelled from school for good" (bk. 6, chap. 6)

Levin finds the Shcherbatsky element—Kitty's family—gaining domination on his estate, and he is annoyed that Stiva brings with him an unknown guest, Veslovsky. Levin's displeasure begins to spread. It is, on a very small and comic scale, like Kitty's sense of defilement after Vronsky's desertion or Anna's final vision of corruption before her suicide. The deep, pervasive feelings of these characters shape and color their world. The process can be ludicrous when it is now awesome; and Levin rather preposterously sees falsehood everywhere. Dolly doesn't really believe in Stiva's love even if she looks pleased that he's there; Koznyshev only pretends to like Oblonsky. Varenka is a plaster saint with her eye on a marriage partner. And Kitty is clearly flirting with Veslovsky. The last is more than Levin can endure, and he speaks to Kitty of the "horror and the comic absurdity" of his situation. Unlike Vronsky, she is "glad of the force of love for her which found expression in his jealousy." With her reassurance Levin takes Stiva and Veslovsky on a shooting party, where Levin finds his recovered spirits lowered again by their frivolity and by Veslovsky's clumsiness. Nothing goes right until finally Levin goes off by himself and brings down his birds. But Levin can have no peace until he sends Veslovsky packing.

The principal contrast of the sixth part hinges on Dolly's visit to Anna and Vronsky. Her sudden release, the children left behind, from responsibilities and concerns leaves her, during the ride, free to think about her life, to enjoy a measure of self-pity and then to daydream about a life like Anna's: "She wants to live. God put that need into our hearts. Quite possibly I should have done the same." A "mischievous smile wrinkled her lips, chiefly because while thinking of Anna's love affair, she conjured up parallel with it an almost identical love affair with an imaginary composite man who was in love with her. Like Anna, she confessed everything to her husband. And Oblonsky's astonishment and embarrassment at the news of her unfaithfulness made her smile." For a moment Dolly, of all people, brings Emma Bovary before us. "As is quite often the case," Tolstoy observes, "with women of unimpeachable moral conduct who are rather tired of the monotony of a virtuous life, she not only condoned from afar an illicit love affair but even envied it." In Dolly's case, the effect upon Stiva must count for much.

But while Dolly finds Anna more beautiful than ever, she comes to see Anna's unhappiness as well, her inability to love her daughter, her use of contraception (a new and shocking idea for Dolly, who dreads another pregnancy), and a little court where he is surrounded by a respectful cabinet and where he plays at life again (as he has in Italy with painting), now building a hospital. Dolly is disenchanted. The room she is given reminds her in its luxury "of the best hotels abroad." Everything in it is new and expensive, not least the the best hotels abroad." Everything in it is new and expensive, not least the "smart lady's maid" before whom Dolly is ashamed to display her "patched dressing jacket," proud as she has been of the "patches and darns" at home. She is surprised to find everyone busily at play, "grown-up people carrying on a children's game in the absence of children." Dolly feels as if she is "taking part in a theatrical performance with better actors than herself" and as if her own performance is spoiling the show. Anna is an assiduous hostess, creating unity among her guests, putting up with Veslovsky's flirtation. But Anna regrets Dolly's leaving; for the feelings that Dolly has raised, however painful, Anna recognizes as "the best part of her inner self" and a part that is being "rapidly smothered by the life she [is] leading."

Among the topics discussed at Vronsky's table is the value of rural councils and magistrates. Dolly cites Levin's scorn for these public institutions, and Vronsky replies with a vigor meant to defend his own interest in them as well. Anna observes that Vronsky has already become, in the six months they have spent on his estate, a member of five or six such institutions. "And

I fear," she adds, "that with such a multiplicity of official duties, the whole thing will become a mere form." There is asperity in her tone; clearly she resents Vronsky's frequent absences to attend these meetings, just as he feels the need to assert his freedom by going. Tolstoy treats the electoral meetings at Kashin as an ugly farce, which Levin loathes but Vronsky greatly enjoys. Vronsky, in fact, resolves to stand himself in three years if he and Anna are married by then, "just as when winning a prize at the races he felt like taking the jockey's place himself next time." The meetings at Kashin present a world of rhetoric and political manipulation. Vronsky is pleased by the "charming good form" he finds in the provinces. Only "the crazy fellow who was married to Kitty Shcherbatsky" had talked a lot of nonsense "with rabid animosity." Perhaps the typical figure at such an occasion is the amiable Sviazhsky, who stands for so much of the world Tolstoy is presenting in the novel: "Sviazhsky was one of those people who always amazed Levin because their extremely logical, though never original, ideas were kept in a watertight compartment and had no influence whatever on their extremely definite and stable lives, which went on quite independently and almost always diametrically opposed to them." Whenever Levin presses Sviazhsky on a point that reveals an inconsistency, he sees a "momentary expression of alarm in Sviazhsky's eyes which he had noticed before whenever he had tried to penetrate beyond the reception rooms of Sviazhsky's mind." When Levin is troubled by his own insincerity or his failure to face the truth in matters of religion, it is with the feeling that there is "something vague and unclean in his soul." He sees himself in the position "for which he found fault with his friend Sviazhsky."

When Levin finally meets Anna in Moscow, he is altogether charmed by her seriousness, her beauty, and her intelligence. After a day of largely senseless talk, he is moved by her naturalness and lack of self-consciousness. Levin is moved to make a witticism about French art, which has had so far to go in its return to realism: "They saw poetry in the very fact that they did not lie." Anna's face lights up with pleasure. What gives the episode its sadness is not Kitty's jealousy afterwards, but the disclosure that Anna has "done all she could . . . to arouse in Levin a feeling of love." Seductiveness is perhaps the only behavior she allows herself any more with Vronsky, and with other men as a matter of course. The obvious contrast is with Natasha at the close of *War and Peace*:

> She took no pains with her manners or with delicacy of speech, or with her toilet. . . . She felt that the allurements instinct had formerly taught her to use would now be merely ridiculous in

the eyes of her husband. . . . She felt that her unity with her husband was not maintained by the poetic feelings that had attracted
him to her, but by something else—indefinite but firm as the bond
between her own body and soul.

(epilogue #1)

At the end we see Anna surrendering to powers of destruction, in her savage
torture of herself and Vronsky, in her sad effort to stir the pitying Kitty
to jealousy. Her world fills with hatred and disgust; everyone she sees is vicious
or filthy. The breakdown of mind creates a stream of consciousness, and the
rage of her last hours is the form her vitality takes. Unlike her husband,
who finds consolation in fashionable superstition, she finds herself outside
all forms of life.

In the last part of the novel, at first suppressed, Tolstoy shows the
mindless rush of Slavic patriotism and war hysteria. We enter that stream
with Koznyshev when his book wins ridicule and early oblivion. He turns
to the Slav question and the Serbo-Turkish war. He sees the excitement as
"frivolous and ridiculous," but he admires its power. "The soul of the nation,"
as he puts it, has "become articulate." And so the intellectual devotes himself
to a "great cause and forgot to think about things in his book" (bk. 8, chap.
1). Vronsky has volunteered to fight for Serbia, taking a whole squadron
at his own expense and evidently looking for death. Oblonsky has come into
his long-sought post and is giving a farewell party for another volunteer,
the unspeakable Veslovsky. Only Levin stands outside this new whirl of
mindlessness, hoping to solve his own problems, insisting that war in itself
is evil. "It's not only a question of sacrificing oneself," he observes to his
brother, "but of killing Turks." In reply Koznyshev glibly cites, "I came
not to send peace but a sword," quoting "the passage from the Gospels that
had always perplexed Levin more than any other, just as if it were the most
comprehensible thing in the world" (bk. 8, chap. 16).

Tolstoy seems to reverse George Eliot's movement, as we see it in
Dorothea Brooke's coming to awareness, moving outward from the self to
include the multifarious and independent world. For Tolstoy the hero must
recover the immediate. To borrow Wittgenstein's terms again, "The aspects
of things that are most important for us are hidden because of their simplicity and familiarity." What Tolstoy's heroes must uncover, in short, is the
framework itself of which Isaiah Berlin has written; they must dissolve false
problems and find their way back to what they have always known. The
emphasis must rest then upon the forms of life which we overlook or distort
or deny, and those forms may be as far back as we can or should go. The

language-game rests in the end upon our activities: "it is not based on grounds. It is not reasonable (or unreasonable). It is there—like our life." "What has to be accepted, the given, is—so one could say—*forms of life*."

Characters like Anna are tragic figures because, for reasons that are admirable, they cannot live divided lives or survive through repression. We can see throughout the last part of the novel how profoundly Anna feels the need to hold Vronsky's love since theirs is not a life given shape by institutional forms—it has no necessities but their happiness, and there are no forms within which to make their love a sanctity. There seems no clear line at last between Anna's wish to believe in Vronsky's love and her readiness to believe that it no longer exists. The torture she inflicts is a reflex of self-pity she begins to suffer, and there are moments when she seems irrationally to wish to be proved right by Vronsky's rejection of her love. We sense this in her despair. Yet before she throws herself under the train, Anna crosses herself. And the familiar gesture, one of the forms of her early life, arouses a series of memories of her childhood and girlhood until "the darkness that enveloped everything for her was torn apart, and for an instant life presented itself to her with all its bright past joys" (bk. 7, chap. 31).

Chronology

1828	Lev Nikolaevich Tolstoy born August 28 at Yasnaya Polyana, his father's estate, eighty miles from Moscow.

1828 Lev Nikolaevich Tolstoy born August 28 at Yasnaya Polyana, his father's estate, eighty miles from Moscow.

1830 Tolstoy's mother dies.

1837 Tolstoy's father dies.

1841 Upon the death of their guardian, Alexandra Osten-Saken, the Tolstoy children move to Kazan.

1844 Tolstoy enters Kazan University in the Department of Eastern Languages but transfers to the Faculty of Law the following year.

1847 Leaves the University without graduating and returns to Yasnaya Polyana, where he attempts a program of social reform directed at the peasants.

1851 Goes to the Caucasus with his eldest brother Nikolai to serve as a volunteer in the army.

1852–53 Enlists officially in the army. *Childhood* published in the *Contemporary*. During campaigns in the Caucasus, Tolstoy writes *Boyhood* and stories of army life. Outbreak of the Crimean War.

1854 Tolstoy visits western Europe. Writes "Lucerne." *Youth* published in the *Contemporary*.

1855 Writes *Sevastopol Sketches*.

1856 Death of Tolstoy's brother Dmitri. Tolstoy contemplates marrying Valerya Arseneva. Resigns from army and returns to Yasnaya Polyana. *The Two Hussars* published in the *Contemporary*.

1857 Tolstoy visits western Europe. Writes "Lucerne." *Youth* published in the *Contemporary*.

1859 *Family Happiness* and *Three Deaths* published; critical reception is less enthusiastic than for his earlier works. Founds an experimental school for peasant children at Yasnaya Polyana.

1860 Tolstoy leaves for western Europe. Death of his brother Nikolai.

1861 Tolstoy returns to Russia. Publishes *Yasnaya Polyana*, an educational journal. Quarrels with Turgenev, challenging him to a duel. Appointed District Arbiter of the Peace. Resumes school work at Yasnaya Polyana.

1862 Resigns as Arbiter. Marries Sofya Andreevna Bers, daughter of a court physician. Closes Yasnaya Polyana school.

1863 Publishes *The Cossacks*. The first of his thirteen children born.

1863–69 Tolstoy writes and publishes *War and Peace*.

1870–72 Begins a novel about Peter the Great, never finished. Reopens school. While reading Pushkin, he is inspired with an idea for a new novel.

1873–77 Writes *Anna Karenina*, which is serialized in the *Russian Herald*. Despite favorable critical reactions, Tolstoy expresses deep dissatisfaction with the novel and confesses having great trouble writing it. He quarrels with publisher Katkov, who refuses to print the epilogue to the novel because of its political content.

1878 Reconciliation between Tolstoy and Turgenev. Tolstoy's great moral crisis leads him into a period of intense theological study and questioning.

1882 Publishes *A Confession*; writes *What I Believe*.

1884 *What I Believe* banned.

1885 Writes stories for Chertkov's *The Intermediary*.

1886 *The Death of Ivan Ilych* published. Tolstoy's play *The Power of Darkness* offends the Tsar, and its performance is forbidden.

1889 *The Kreutzer Sonata* published.

1893–96 *The Kingdom of God Is within You*, *Christianity and Patriotism*, *Reason and Religion*, *Religion and Morality*, *Master and Man*, *How to Read the Gospels*.

1898 Publishes *What Is Art?*

1899 Publishes *Resurrection*, which he has been writing for ten years.

1901 Excommunicated by the Holy Synod of the Russian Orthodox Church. *Reply to the Synod's Edict*.

1904–5 Finishes *Hadji Murad*. Writes *Alyosha the Pot* and *The Posthumous Notes of Fyodor Kuzmich*. Beginning of Russo-Japanese War and the 1905 Revolution.

1908–9 Finishes *I Cannot Be Silent!*, a protest against the hanging of the 1905 revolutionaries. Growing quarrels between Tolstoy and his wife.

1910 Tolstoy leaves his wife and is taken ill on the train. He dies on the platform of the Astapovo train station on November 7.

Contributors

HAROLD BLOOM, Sterling Professor of the Humanities at Yale University, is the author of *The Anxiety of Influence, Poetry and Repression*, and many other volumes of literary criticism. His forthcoming study, *Freud: Transference and Authority*, attempts a full-scale reading of all of Freud's major writings. A MacArthur Prize Fellow, he is general editor of five series of literary criticism published by Chelsea House. During 1987–88, he was appointed Charles Eliot Norton Professor of Poetry at Harvard University.

JOHN BAYLEY is Wharton Professor of English Literature at Oxford University. His books include *The Uses of Division, Selected Essays, Romantic Survival, Shakespeare and Tragedy*, and *Pushkin: A Comparative Commentary.*

ROBERT LOUIS JACKSON teaches in the Department of Slavic Studies at Yale University. He is the author of several works on Dostoevsky.

WILLIS KONICK is Associate Professor of Russian Literature at the University of Washington in Seattle.

EDWARD WASIOLEK is Professor of Russian and Comparative Literature at the University of Chicago. He is the author of *Dostoevsky: The Major Fiction.*

MAIRE JAANUS KURRIK teaches in the English Department at Barnard College and is the author of *Literature and Negation.*

MARTIN PRICE is Sterling Professor of English at Yale University. His books include *Swift's Rhetorical Art: A Study in Structure and Meaning, To the Palace of Wisdom: Studies in Order and Energy from Dryden to Blake*, and a number of edited volumes on literature of the seventeenth, eighteenth, and nineteenth centuries.

127

Bibliography

Alexandrov, Vladimir E. "Relative Time in *Anna Karenina*." *The Russian Review* 41 (1982): 159–68.

Arnold, Matthew. "Count Leo Tolstoy." In *The Last Word*, edited by R. H. Super. Ann Arbor: University of Michigan Press, 1977.

Bayley, John. *Tolstoy and the Novel*. London: Chatto & Windus, 1966.

Benson, Ruth Grego. *Women in Tolstoy: The Ideal and the Erotic*. Urbana: University of Illinois Press, 1973.

Black, Michael. "Anna Karenina and the Cost of Self-Fulfillment." In *The Literature of Fidelity*. London: Chatto & Windus, 1975.

Blackmur, R. P. "The Dialectic of Incarnation: Tolstoy's *Anna Karenina*." In *Eleven Essays in the European Novel*. New York: Harcourt, Brace & World, 1964.

Blumberg, Edwina Jannie. "Tolstoy and the English Novel: A Note on *Middlemarch* and *Anna Karenina*." *Slavic Review* 30 (1971): 561–69.

Boyd, A. F. "Leo Tolstoy and *Anna Karenina*." In *Aspects of the Russian Novel*. London: Chatto & Windus, 1972.

Calder, Angus. "Man, Woman, and Male Woman: Tolstoy's Anna and After." In *Russia Discovered: Nineteenth-Century Fiction from Pushkin to Chekhov*. New York: Barnes & Noble, 1976.

Call, Paul. "Anna Karenina's Crime and Punishment." *Mosaic* 1 (1967): 94–102.

Cary, Joyce. *Art and Reality: Ways of the Creative Process*. New York: Harper & Row, 1958.

Christian, Reginald Frank. "The Passage of Time in *Anna Karenina*." *The Slavonic and East European Review* 45 (1967): 207–10.

———. "The Problem of Tendentiousness in *Anna Karenina*." *Canadian Slavonic Papers* 21, no. 3 (1979): 276–88.

———. *Tolstoy: A Critical Introduction*. Cambridge: Cambridge University Press, 1969.

———. *Tolstoy's* War and Peace: *A Study*. Oxford: Oxford University Press, 1962.

Comings, Andrew G. "Tolstoy's *Anna Karenina*: The Problem of Form." In *Occasional Papers in Language, Literature, and Linguistics*. Athens: Modern Languages Department, Ohio University, 1973.

Davie, Donald, ed. *Russian Literature and Modern English Fiction*. Chicago: University of Chicago Press, 1965.

Demetz, Peter, Thomas Greene, and Lowry Nelson, Jr., eds. *The Disciplines of Criticism*. New Haven: Yale University Press, 1968.

Ducusin, Dionisio S. "The Experience of Nothingness in *Anna Karenina*: A Study of the Existential Differences of Anna and Alexandrovich." *St. Louis University Research Journal* 6 (1975): 293–305.

Egan, David R. *Leo Tolstoy: An Annotated Bibliography of English-Language Sources to 1978.* Metuchen, N.J.: Scarecrow, 1979.

Feuer, Katherine B. "Stiva." In *Russian Literature and American Critics*, edited by Kenneth B. Brostrom. Ann Arbor: University of Michigan Press, 1984.

Flint, Martha M. "The Epigraph of *Anna Karenina.*" *PMLA* 80 (1965): 461–62.

French, A. L. "*Anna Karenina*: Tolstoy's 'Toryism.' " *The Critical Review* (Canberra) 22 (1980): 21–31.

Friedman, Simon. "Detail and Accident in *Anna Karenina.*" *Proceedings of the Pacific Northwest Conference on Foreign Languages* 26, no. 1 (1975): 164–66.

Garnett, Edward. *Tolstoy: His Life and Writings.* London: Constable; New York: Houghton Mifflin, 1914.

Garrard, John G. "Old Wine in New Bottles: The Legacy of Lermontov." In *Poetica Slavica: Essays in Honor of Zbigniew Folejewski*, edited by J. D. Clayton et. al. Ottawa: University of Ottawa Press, 1981.

Gifford, Henry. *Leo Tolstoy: A Critical Anthology.* Harmondsworth, England: Penguin, 1971.

Gorodetsky, Nadezhda. "*Anna Karenina.*" *The Slavonic and East European Review* 24 (1946): 121–26.

Greene, Gayle. "Women, Character, and Society in Tolstoy's *Anna Karenina.*" *Frontiers* 2, no. 1 (Spring 1977): 106–25.

Greenwood, E. B. "Tragedy, Contingency, and the Meaning of Life in *Anna Karenina.*" In *Tolstoy: The Comprehensive Vision.* New York: St. Martin's, 1975.

———. "The Unity of *Anna Karenina.*" *Landfall* (New Zealand) 15 (1961): 124–34.

Grossman, Joan Delaney. "Tolstoy's Portrait of Anna: Keystone in the Arch." *Criticism* 18 (1976): 1–14.

Gunn, Elizabeth. *A Daring Coiffeur: Reflections on* War and Peace *and* Anna Karenina. London: Chatto & Windus, 1971.

Gustafson, Richard F. *Leo Tolstoy, Resident and Stranger: A Study in Fiction and Theology.* Princeton: Princeton University Press, 1986.

Hardy, Barbara. "Form and Freedom: Tolstoy's *Anna Karenina.*" In *The Appropriate Form: An Essay on the Novel*, 174–211. London: Athlone, 1964.

Holderness, G. "Tolstoi and Art." *Durham University Journal* 73, no. 2 (June 1981): 135–46.

Jahn, Gary R. "The Image of the Railroad in *Anna Karenina.*" *Slavic and East European Journal* 25 (1981): 1–10.

———. "A Note on the Organization of Part I of *Anna Karenina.*" *Canadian-American Slavic Studies* 16, no. 1 (1982): 82–86.

———. "The Unity of *Anna Karenina.*" *The Russian Review* 41 (1982): 144–58.

Johnson, Doris V. "The Autobiographical Heroine in *Anna Karenina.*" *University of Hartford Studies in Literature* 11 (1979): 111–22.

Jones, Malcolm V., ed. "Problems of Communication in *Anna Karenina.*" In *New Essays on Tolstoy.* Cambridge: Cambridge University Press, 1978.

Jones, Peter. "Action and Passion in *Anna Karenina.*" In *Philosophy and the Novel.* Oxford: Clarendon, 1975.

Jones, T. Robert. "*Anna Karenina* and the Tragic Genre." *Melbourne Slavonic Studies* 4 (1970): 57–67.

Jones, W. G. "George Eliot's *Adam Bede* and Tolstoy's Conception of *Anna Karenina*." *The Modern Language Review* 61, (1966): 473–81.

Kantak, V. Y. "The Dirty Old Peasant of *Anna Karenina*." *The Literary Criterion* (Mysore, India) 17, no. 3 (1982): 11–24.

Klimenko, Michael. "*Anna Karenina* Seen as an Expression of Schopenhauer's *Willie zum Leben*." *Proceedings of the Pacific Northwest Conference on Foreign Languages* 22 (1970): 271–78.

Knowles, Anthony V. "Russian Views of *Anna Karenina*, 1875–1878." *Slavic and East European Journal* 22 (1978): 301–12.

————, ed. *Tolstoy: The Critical Heritage.* London: Routledge & Kegan Paul, 1978.

Larkin, Maurice. "Experience versus the Intellect: Tolstoy." In *Man and Society in Nineteenth-Century Realism.* Totowa, N.J.: Rowman & Littlefield, 1977.

Lavrin, Janko. *Tolstoy: An Approach.* New York: Macmillan, 1946.

Leavis, F. R. *Anna Karenina and Other Essays.* London: Chatto & Windus, 1967.

————. "*Anna Karenina*: Thought and Significance in a Great Creative Work." *The Cambridge Quarterly* 1, no. 1 (Winter 1955–56): 5–27.

Ledkovsky, Marina. "Dolly Oblonskaia as a Structural Device in *Anna Karenina*." *Canadian-American Slavic Studies* 12 (1978): 543–48.

Leon, Derrick. *Tolstoy: His Life and Work.* London: Routledge & Kegan Paul, 1944.

Lyons, John. "Pronouns of Address in *Anna Karenina*: The Stylistics of Bilingualism and the Impossibility of Translation." In *Studies in English Linguistics: For Randolph Quirk,* edited by Sidney Greenbaum, Geoffrey Leech, and Jan Svartvik. New York: Longmans, 1980.

Mann, Thomas. "*Anna Karenina*." In *Essays by Thomas Mann,* translated by H. T. Lowe-Porter. New York: Vintage, 1957.

Matlaw, Ralph E., ed. *Tolstoy: A Collection of Critical Essays.* Englewood Cliffs, N.J.: Prentice-Hall, 1967.

Maude, Alymer. *Leo Tolstoy and His Works.* New York: Oxford University Press, 1931.

Mihajlov, Mihajlo. *Underground Notes.* Translated by Maria Mihajlov Ivusic and Christopher W. Ivusic. New Rochelle, N.Y.: Caratzas Brothers, 1982.

Muchnic, Helen. *Russian Writers: Notes and Essays.* New York: Random House, 1971.

Nabokov, Vladimir. "Leo Tolstoy: *Anna Karenina*." In *Lectures on Russian Literature.* Edited by Fredson Bowers. New York: Harcourt Brace Jovanovich, 1981.

Pearson, Irene. "The Social and Moral Roles of Food in *Anna Karenina*." *Journal of Russian Studies* 48 (1984): 10–19.

Pursglove, Michael. "The Smiles of *Anna Karenina*." *Slavic and East European Journal* 17 (1973): 42–48.

Redpath, Theodore. *Tolstoy.* London: Bowes & Bowes, 1969.

Reeve, Franklin D. "*Anna Karenina*." In *The Russian Novel.* New York: McGraw-Hill, 1966.

Schultze, Sydney. "The Chapter in *Anna Karenina*." *Russian Literature Triquarterly*, no. 10 (1974): 351–59.

————. "Notes on Imagery and Motifs in *Anna Karenina*." *Russian Language Triquarterly*, no. 1 (1971): 366–74.

Shklovskii, Viktor Borisovich. *Leo Tolstoy.* Translated by Olga Shartse. Moscow: Progress, 1978.

Simmons, Ernest J. "*Anna Karenina*." In *Introduction to Tolstoy's Writings.* Chicago: University of Chicago Press, 1968.

————. *Leo Tolstoy*. New York: Vintage, 1960.

————. "My Hero is Truth." In *Introduction to Russian Realism*. Bloomington: Indiana University Press, 1965.

Simpson, Mark. "Dolokhov and Vronsky: Two of Tolstoy's Officers and Their Background." *New Zealand Slavonic Journal* 2 (1980): 49–58.

Slade, Tony. "*Anna Karenina* and the Family Ideal." *The Southern Review*, no. 1 (1963): 85–90.

Speirs, Logan. *Tolstoy and Chekhov*. Cambridge: Cambridge University Press, 1971.

Spence, Gordon William. "Levin." In *Tolstoy the Ascetic*. New York: Barnes & Noble, 1967.

Stenbock-Fermor, Elisabeth. *The Architecture of* Anna Karenina: *A History of Its Structure, Writing and Message*. Lisse, Belgium: Peter de Ridder Press, 1975.

Stevens, Martin. "A Source for Frou-Frou in *Anna Karenina*." *Comparative Literature* 24 (1972): 63–71.

Stewart, David H. "*Anna Karenina*: The Dialectic of Prophecy." *PMLA* 79 (1964): 266–82.

Terras, Victor, ed. *American Contributions to the Eighth International Congress of Slavists, Volume II*. Columbus, Ohio: Slavica, 1978.

Trilling, Lionel. "*Anna Karenina*." In *The Opposing Self*. New York: Viking, 1955.

Troyat, Henri. *Tolstoy*. New York: Doubleday, 1967.

Walsh, Harry Hill. "A Buddhistic Leitmotif in *Anna Karenina*." *Canadian-American Slavic Studies* 11, no. 4 (Winter 1977): 561–67.

Wasiolek, Edward. *Tolstoy's Major Fiction*. Chicago: University of Chicago Press, 1978.

Wierzbicka, Anna. "The Semantic Structure of Words for Emotions." In *Slavic Poetics: Essays in honor of Kiril Taranovsky*, edited by Roman Jakobson, C. H. von Schooneveld, and Dean S. Worth. The Hague: Mouton, 1973.

Williams, Raymond. "Social and Personal Tragedy: Tolstoy and Lawrence." In *Modern Tragedy*. Stanford: Stanford University Press, 1966.

Yeon, Jeom Suk. "Death-in-life and Life-in-death Resulting from Anxiety in *Anna Karenina*." *St. Louis University Research Journal* 11 (1980): 338–82.

Zweers, A. F. "Is There Only One Anna Karenina?" *Canadian Slavonic Papers* 11, no. 2 (Summer 1969): 272–81.

Acknowledgments

"Anna Karenina" (originally entitled " 'This novel . . .' *Anna Karenina"*) by John Bayley from *Tolstoy and the Novel* by John Bayley, © 1966 by John Bayley. Reprinted by permission of the author and Chatto & Windus, Inc.

"Chance and Design in *Anna Karenina"* by Robert Louis Jackson from *The Disciplines of Criticism*, edited by Peter Demetz, Thomas Greene, and Lowry Nelson, Jr., © 1968 by Yale University. Reprinted by permission of Yale University Press.

"Tolstoy's Underground Woman: A Study of *Anna Karenina"* by Willis Konick from *Russian and Slavic Literature*, edited by Richard Freeborn, © 1976 by Slavica Publishers, Inc. Reprinted by permission of the author and Slavica Publishers, Inc.

"Anna Karenina: The Two Novels" (originally entitled *"Anna Karenina"*) by Edward Wasiolek from *Tolstoy's Major Fiction* by Edward Wasiolek, © 1978 by the University of Chicago. Reprinted by permission of the University of Chicago Press.

"Tolstoy's *Anna Karenina:* The Self's Negativity" (originally entitled "Tolstoy's *Anna Karenina"*) by Maire Jaanus Kurrik from *Literature and Negation* by Maire Jaanus Kurrik, © 1979 by Columbia University Press. Reprinted by permission of Columbia University Press.

"Tolstoy and the Forms of Life: 'Inexorable Law' " by Martin Price from *Forms of Life: Character and Moral Imagination in the Novel* by Martin Price, © 1983 by Yale University. Reprinted by permission of the author and Yale University Press.

Index

Anatole (*War and Peace*), 64

Anna Karenina, 3, 9, 18–19, 33–35, 41;
alienation of, 42, 43, 52–53; and
beauty, 56–57; characterization of,
34–35, 41; coexistence vs. isolation
of, 102–3; conflicting loyalties of,
53–54; consciousness vs. body of,
27, 36, 37, 40, 41, 103, 105–6;
contraction of life of, 118; contradictory nature of, 35, 48–53, 67;
cruelty of, 57; cyclical nature of
life of, 59–60; death wish of, 77;
and definition of love, 26, 54, 56;
degeneration of, 76, 82–83, 86–87,
118, 122; despair of, 16, 27, 28,
39; destructive drives of, 88,
89–90, 122; and divorce from
Karenin, 80–81; dreams of, 5;
effect of relationship with Vronsky
on, 53–54; enjoyment of life of,
27, 103, 105–6; and erotic
experience as loss of self, 103–4,
105–6; and feelings towards
Karenin, 49–50, 57, 70, 75, 77–78;
and feelings toward her son,
58–59; 78–79, 81; and feelings
toward Vronsky, 20, 23, 24, 26,
59, 67–68, 72–73, 79, 81, 84–86,
103, 104–6; in first draft, 7–9,
12–13, 15; gloominess of, 40; at
horse race, 18–20, 74–75; illness
of, 28, 30; immediateness of,
13–14; impenetrability of, 15;
impulsiveness of, 12; inconsistent
behavior of, 35, 48–53; independence of, 22, 36; intensity
of, 3–5; isolation of, 20, 27–28; in
Italy, 78–79; jealousy of, 20; and
lack of sense of past, 51, 57–60;
last day of, 81; and Levin, 93–94;
and likeness to Stiva Oblonsky,
7–8, 9–10; manipulative behavior
of, 46–48; moral consciousness of,
42–43; as mother, 58–59, 78–79,
81; motives of, 55–56, 78–80, 84,
85; near death experience of, 77,
105; obliviousness of, 111–13; at
the opera, 79–80; passion of, 12,
13, 69–70, 75–76; physicality of,
27, 36, 37, 40, 41, 103, 105–6;
reason and unreason behind,
111–12; and relationship with
Karenin, 49–50, 57, 70, 88–89;
and relationship to self, 103–5; and
relationship with society, 27, 43,
79; and relationship with Vronsky,
40, 49–51, 54–55, 63, 66–67,
71–73, 75, 80; resoluteness of,
35–36; and return to Petersburg,
15–16, 67–68; self-awareness of,
60, 68; self-hatred of, 56; shame
of, 4–5; and solitude, 22, 36;
suffering of, 73–74, 78, 79–80, 84;
suicide of, 1, 18, 26, 31, 38,
41–44, 66, 82–83, 85, 103, 105;
tragedy of, 5–6, 40–44, 123; on
the train, 68–70; at the train
station, 82; transformation of,